Classic
American Pickups

BIG
STONE
PASS

RAIL ROAD
CROSSING
STOP
Ford

ROLET

TISANA
COLORADO

CHEVROLET

Classic
American Pickups

MADE IN AMERICA FROM 1910 TO THE PRESENT

John Carroll

Photographs by Garry Stuart

THUNDER BAY
P·R·E·S·S

Published in the United States by
Thunder Bay Press
An imprint of the Advantage Publishers Group
5880 Oberlin Drive, San Diego, CA 92121-4794
www.advantagebooksonline.com

1 2 3 4 5 00 01 02 03 04

All correspondence concerning the content of this volume should be addressed to Salamander Books Ltd.

ISBN 1-57145-274-5

Library of Congress Cataloging-in-Publication Data available.

Credits
Editor Charlotte Davies
Designer John Heritage
All photographs by Garry Stuart
Film set: SX Composing Ltd, England
Reproduction: P+W Graphics, Singapore
Printed in Spain

Acknowledgements
Both author and photographer are indebted to Dale Richards and Martha Richmond of Greeley, Colorado for their assistance with this book and to the owners of all the trucks featured herein. Everyone is indebted to Henry Ford and the others who pioneered what is, without doubt, one of the coolest forms of four-wheeled transport around.

Additional captions
page 1
A '46 Dodge grille detail
pages 2-3
A Chevrolet stepside truck
pages 4-5
A street-rodded Ford at a railroad crossing
pages 6-7
Chevrolet truck grille and headlights detail
pages 8-9
Contemporary Model A Ford street rod truck
page 10
1959 Chevrolet Apache fleetside truck

Endpapers
Floyd Dahl's 1933 V8 Ford truck

CONTENTS

FORD

INTRODUCTION

Left: *George Yackey worked for Case and bought this Ford F-1 truck new in 1949. From then until 1971 it was used as a farm machinery service truck. The Colorado summer sunshine has faded the paint from its original red to burnt orange.*

THE PICKUP TRUCK is inextricably linked to the development of America itself. As surely as the horse and the shovel, so the pickup truck has helped shape a land and a nation. The history of the truck starts with the transition from horse to the internal combustion engine as the prime source of motive power. Where the history will end is unknown but it's no accident that there is a 1936 Ford truck in the *Star Trek Voyager* TV series. The program-makers, looking for something that encapsulated twentieth century America featured a pickup truck drifting through space. This gives an indication of how far the pickup has worked its way into the American consciousness.

As well as having shaped America, the history of the pickup can be seen as a microcosm of the history of the twentieth century. There were pickups working on farms on the day in the spring of 1917 that the *Lusitania* was torpedoed off Ireland, and America entered the war. There were Chevy pickups hauling bootleg liquor through the Prohibition era, Ford pickups hauling rapidly devaluing goods after the 1929 crash on the New York Stock Exchange and a beat up truck hauled Tom Jaud and his family west to California. There were pickups engaged in the construction of the Hoover and Grand Coulee dams as America worked its way out of the Great Depression. Pickups were carrying service personnel about their business on the day that the skies above Pearl Harbor filled with Mitsubishi Zeroes, and Dodges and Jeeps splashed ashore on Pacific Islands. Dodges and GMCs hauled the GIs of the Allied Army across Europe. Trucks had a place in the changed postwar world too; the guy who delivered parts from the local Case dealer brought tractor parts out to the farm in one of them new Fords. Trucks evolved in response to the gas crisis of the early seventies, and in the eighties and nineties trucks were decreed to be cool and a lifestyle evolved around them. Slammed minis and outrageously tall 4x4s vied for attention at shows while mainstream pickups became ever more luxurious and competed with sport utilities and station wagons in dealers' showrooms across America.

Each chapter of this book opens with a quote that sets the pickup truck in the context of that particular decade. It's no surprise that pickups are mentioned so often, just as it is unsurprising that vintage and classic trucks are still being driven, restored, and street rodded as well as being regarded with such affection. There's no doubt about it, a pickup is a whole lot more than "just another means of transportation."

Above *Through a succession of careful owners, this 1925 Model TT one-ton closed cab truck has survived almost as it was when new. Note the wooden spoked wheels and grain-carrying load bed.*

No sooner had the three trucks left town than Rusk appeared in his pickup, accompanied by Dewey Kimbro, and when the new newpaper editor shouted: What's Up? Rusk cried back: We're spudding in an oil well.

TEXAS. JAMES MICHENER (1985).

BEGINNINGS

In Texas on January 10, 1901 something happened that helped the internal combustion engine progress ahead of horses, steam and electricity as the primary source of power for vehicles. The huge Spindletop oilfield produced crude oil for the first time on that date and from the liquid black gold came kerosene, paraffin, naphtha and later, crucially, gasoline. The early history of the pickup truck is inextricably intertwined with that of the first automobiles. In exactly the same way as there had been horse-drawn vehicles for carrying people and horse-drawn vehicles for carrying goods, from the earliest days of the motor industry there would be machines designed with both these separate purposes in mind.

As early as 1900 there were four large automobile shows held in the US. In this year shows were held in Bedford, Connecticut, Chicago, Illinois, Trenton, New Jersey and at New York's Madison Square Garden. The latter event was by far the largest featuring 300 vehicles from around 40 manufacturers and was run under the auspices of the Auto Club of America. The now more well known Automobile Association of America was founded in 1902.

Oldsmobile is acknowledged to have built the first factory specifically intended for motor vehicle production in 1901. Simply it was forced to rebuild its factory following a disastrous fire which all but destroyed the business. In the wake of the fire, in order to resume production it started sub-contracting for many of the components used in its production of cars, something that is now widespread in the auto industry worldwide. In the 1900s the US population numbered approximately 76 million people of whom the majority lived in rural locations. Roads existed but only 150,000 miles of them could be described as "improved" at the time. Improved did not mean surfaced as only 150 miles of the improved total were actually hard surfaced.

Many of the companies who would flourish in the early years of auto manufacture were already established making related items such as agricultural machines.

The International Harvester Corporation (IHC) had its beginnings in the McCormick reaper of 1831 which subsequently led to the formation of IHC in 1902. By 1907 the company began production of commercial vehicles and vehicles such as the Auto-Wagon which offered a choice of panel truck and grain box bodies were being produced. Through the remainder of the decade the company went on to produce a range of light trucks including utility wagons and panel trucks but gradually shifted its emphasis wholly to light trucks. A new line of conventional trucks was introduced in 1915 with payloads ranging upward from three quarters of a ton.

Studebaker's involvement with light trucks also pre-dates the advent of the motor vehicle – the company had been manufacturing horse-drawn commercial vehicles in South Bend, Indiana since 1852. Henry and Clem Studebaker had a blacksmith's shop in South Bend where they made wagons for local farmers. From this humble beginning evolved a noted horse-drawn vehicle manufacturing operation and by 1876 the company was a large concern. After experimenting with some early automobile designs and electric propulsion around the turn of the century it finally introduced an internal combustion engine powered automobile in 1902. Studebaker subsequently cooperated with other fledgling manufacturers including the EMF Co and Flanders but by 1914 the company was sufficiently established to introduce a light commercial vehicle of its own, the three-quarter-ton Model Three Delivery Car. This truck was available in two forms, panel or an express delivery, basically a van or a pickup. These machines were powered by an in-line four cylinder engine of 192.4 cubic inch displacement, achieved through a bore and stroke of 3.5 x 5 inches and produced 30 hp. The vehicles remained in production until in 1918 Studebaker discontinued all commercial vehicle production.

The now massive GMC corporation had started in an equally small way; in 1903 William C. Durant took control of Buick and in 1908 founded the General Motors Company which absorbed a number of other early car and truck makers. Starting in 1911, the same year as GM shares were listed on the New York Stock Exchange for the first time, the company's trucks were sold as GMC models. By this time devel-

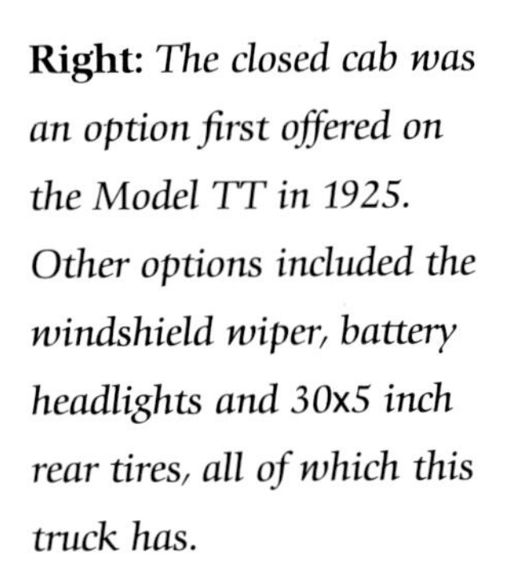

Right: *The closed cab was an option first offered on the Model TT in 1925. Other options included the windshield wiper, battery headlights and 30x5 inch rear tires, all of which this truck has.*

Left: *The Model TT was powered by a 176.7 cu in displacement L-head engine. A choice of Kingston or Holley carburetors were fitted. This engine has had a crack in the cylinder head welded and is original apart from the new Champion sparkplugs – Champion still make plugs for Model Ts.*

Above *The door windows are raised and lowered by means of this leather strap incorporated into the door.*

opments were occurring thick and fast. In 1910 the US auto industry had produced 187,000 vehicles of which 6,000 were trucks and buses and at the New York Auto show that year White Steamer displayed its first gasoline engined truck. Diamond T abandoned car production to concentrate on large trucks.

No account of the first years of the automobile industry would be complete without significant mention of Henry Ford. He was born in 1863 on a farm near Dearborn, Michigan. The farm belonged to his father, William Ford, so Henry grew up with the drudgery of farm work and horse-drawn implements and it was these experiences that fuelled his interest in all things mechanical. By 1893 Henry Ford was an employee of the Edison Illuminating Company in Detroit, Michigan. In his spare time he experimented with internal combustion engines and their potential for vehicles. Henry Ford drove his first four wheeled vehicle, a twin cylinder, four stroke engined, gasoline fuelled quadricycle on June 4th 1896. It had two forward gears and was capable of 10 mph in low and 20 mph in high. The former farmer and skilled mechanic went on to build another car while still in Edison's employ. This was the auto buggy, a tiller steered two cylinder car with planetary gear transmission and chain drive. In 1899 he left the Edison Illuminating Company and founded the Detroit Auto Company which later became the Henry Ford Company. Ford himself eventually left after a disagreement about company strategy. Ford wanted to build low priced machines while his colleagues wanted to build expensive luxury motorcars. Once Ford left the company it was reorganized into the

Right *The Ford script logo is embossed into the running boards of the truck. Diamond pressings give grip when the truck is wet.*

Cadillac Company. In 1902 Ford built an experimental people's car and in June 1903 he was one of the thirteen men who set up the Ford Motor Company with raised capital of $100,000. Ford's experimental Model A represented Ford's investment of $25,000 and in the next few months more than 1,700 of them were sold at $850 each. In 1905 the American Society of Automobile Engineers was formed and Henry Ford was one of the Vice Presidents. This was the time when the proponents of steam and electric cars were falling by the wayside and the internal combustion engine became dominant, hence the importance of oilfields in states such as Texas.

In the 1906-07 sales year, Ford became the world's largest automaker with the manufacture of 8,423 15 hp four cylinder Model N cars that retailed at $550 each. Ford owned 51% of the company's stock and the company turned a profit of $1 million. Henry Ford's reputation was assured. In 1907 the Ford Motor Company built the prototype of what it hoped would be the world's first mass-produced agricultural tractor. In 1905 Ford had offered what it described as the Delivery Car, basically a Model C automobile with a delivery-type body. It was discontinued in 1906 and between then and 1911 the only Ford trucks made were those constructed by converting cars. The Model T Delivery Car was introduced in 1912 and was followed by the Model TT - a Model T Ton, a one-ton capacity truck. There was also a range of Model T Roadster pickups and some specifically constructed panel trucks. At the same time Henry Ford was experimenting with the moving assembly line, reputedly

Below *Decaying in a South Dakota field is this twenties one-ton International Harvester Model S. Note the wood - spoked wheels and opening windshield.*

Left *During the twenties International Harvester used in-line four-cylinder L-head engines for its trucks. Some were made by Waukesha and others by Lycoming.*

inspired by the overhead trolley system used in the beef packing business. As history proved it was a great success and by 1913, 1,000 Model Ts were coming off the line each day.

The official line is that the Ford Motor Company has been making a variety of pickup trucks, more usually referred to simply as "trucks" since 1917, which is when Ford started mass production of a truck. This coincided with the massive demand for trucks following America's involvement in World War One. The main supply of trucks prior to this date came through smaller companies who would fabricate a commercial body on a rolling chassis cab which Ford sold for precisely this purpose. By 1917 the number of small companies who would custom-build truck bodies onto such Ford chassis cabs had multiplied, with the result that some were producing poor quality goods. Ford, no doubt correctly, felt that this was likely to reflect badly on his products so on July 27 1917 the Ford Motor Company announced a one-ton chassis that would form the basis for the company's own truck program. This new chassis was stronger than that for Ford cars and had a two feet longer wheelbase, heavier rear suspension and solid tires on heavy duty wheels. It was referred to as the Model TT after the car from which it was derived.

By the time of the outbreak of World War One motor vehicle production was locked into the American national economy for all time as the motor industry had, by then, produced an estimated $700

Below *The Ford Model A and AA trucks were available as closed cab, open cab, panel truck, and chassis cabs. This is the closed cab Model AA version.*

million worth of vehicles. The wider economic climate was right for the development of the automobile as well. The Federal Aid Road Act encouraged the establishment of state highway departments by offering individual states matching Federal Funds for the creation of better roads. The Dodge brothers started by making automobiles in 1914 and became heavily involved in the manufacture of commercial bodied variants during World War One.

During the war with Mexico a motorized raid on the rebel forces of Pancho Villa was led by George S. Patton Junior, then a lieutenant and a man of whom history would later hear more. General "Black Jack" Pershing was so impressed by the 250 Dodge Cars bought by the US Army and used in this way by his forces during the campaigning in Mexico that he ordered his army staff to use only Dodge Cars and as a result Dodge began to build a variety of commercial vehicles for use as troop carriers, ambulances and light trucks. The Mexican campaign was the first time that the US Army had used motor vehicles. Until this time mobility depended entirely on cavalry, and tactics of the American Civil and Indian wars of years earlier.

On April 6 1917 the United States declared war on Germany. The Democrat President, Woodrow Wilson, made a plea to industry requesting all-out production and by the time of the Armistice in 1918 a considerable number of vehicles had been supplied to the US Army. The first civilian Dodge truck which went on sale in 1917 was basically a civilianized version of the screen-sided panel built for the US Army. Other developments followed that affected the automobile; in 1919 the State of Oregon was the first to introduce a state gasoline tax. A one cent tax was added to the price of every gallon sold. In the same year Washington State allocated $65 million for road construction and across the US the number of road miles now reached approximately three million.

The unpopular 18th Amendment to the US Constitution which prevented the sale and production of alcohol had been introduced in January 1920 and started the Prohibition Era. By then the automobile business was the largest industry in the US. The American road network continued to develop, North to South roads were given odd number numerical designations while East to West ones were given even numbered ones. Warren G. Harding became the first US President to travel by car to his inauguration when he rode in a Packard on March 4 1921. The various manufacturers sought innovative ways to increase sales to the booming but fickle market; for a period another company was involved in the production of Dodge trucks for example. In the year of

Below *This six-wheeled Model AA (6x4) truck used a tandem axle to drive both rear axles. The Model AAs were larger payload versions of the Model A and used stronger components such as pressed steel wheels instead of laced ones.*

Harding's inauguration Dodge made an agreement with a company called Graham to market its trucks (which used Dodge components) through Dodge dealers. By 1923 these were Dodge passenger cars with Graham commercial bodies - an arrangement that endured until 1928. Circumstances changed when Walter P. Chrysler acquired Dodge in June 1928. He changed the name of the trucks back to Dodge and sanctioned the use of a four cylinder Plymouth engine; production of these machines then continued until 1933.

The General Motors Corporation had started light truck production in the second decade of the twentieth century and produced a range of trucks prior to the World War One. Its early models earned a reputation for being both rugged and reliable and during the war the Model 16 One Tonner became the basis for many US Army ambulances. In the years after the war it became the basis for the GMC K-series. GMC acquired Chevrolet during World War One after a period of secretly acquiring GM stock. Another merger followed in 1925 and another would follow in 1943 increasing the company's size each time.

The first pickups from Chevrolet appeared in

Above: *The radiator filter cap also serves as a temperature gauge and the needle can be seen in the vertical position.*

1918, a year in which the company made less than 1,000 in both half- and one-ton capacities. The pickups were however a success and in the following year the company produced in excess of 8,000.

In the early twenties the company installed a variety of outside sourced bodies on its chassis cab trucks in Chevrolet plants. For example the 1922 Chevrolet three-quarter-ton Model G retailed at $650 for the chassis and cowl alone, without the rest of the body. This pattern continued through the twenties with occasional additions to the range such as an all-steel enclosed cab model in 1925 as well as a panel truck in the same year. A new line of IHC trucks introduced in 1921 was known as the S-series. The 'S' prefix designated a "speed truck" and these trucks were capable of 30 mph. Because of the machines' diminutive size and red paintwork the range soon became nicknamed "Red Babies." The IHC trucks were sold through 170 IHC farm equipment dealers where the company's trucks acquired the nickname of "cornbinders".

Sales declined in 1921 as part of an overall economic decline, Henry Ford survived by dropping the price of the Model T to the extent that 55% of cars sold in that year were Model Ts. In 1925 Ford produced the Model T with a pickup body. Other developments around this time included improved lubrication systems, pneumatic tires and a lower steering ratio. The next stage in the development of the Ford trucks was when the designs of cars and commercial vehicles diverged. This was seen as a mixed blessing due to the lessening of spares interchangeability. Chevrolet pulled ahead in terms of sales in 1927 with the best selling truck in America and so the long-running Ford versus Chevrolet rivalry began.

Ford discontinued the long production run of the Model T, affectionately referred to as the "Tin Lizzie," having produced in excess of fifteen million vehicles. The Model T was replaced by the Model A in 1928 and Ford soon regained the sales advantage when the Model A car and the Model AA truck started coming off the production lines. The Ford Model AA, half-ton models were available as both Roadster and closed cab pickups and by 1931 there were 31 different colors of Ford truck available. Although this gave Ford the lead, the Wall Street Crash hit in October 1929 and devastated America's economy. The Crash would lead to the Great Depression which would last into the thirties and see an estimated 13 million Americans out of work by 1932.

By 1928 Chevrolet had become a major threat to Ford's dominance of both the car and truck markets. In the last year of the decade Chevrolet produced its half-millionth truck and introduced an in-line six cylinder engine. Production of GMC trucks had continued through the twenties with engines supplied by companies including Buick who supplied GMC with their six cylinder engines.

Towards the end of the decade GMC offered a truck, the T-11, based on a Pontiac design that had only been offered for a single year and in this initial model even the Pontiac engine was used. A new model, the T-19, was introduced in 1928 and showed that GMC was also developing its truck designs. The T-19 was manufactured in large numbers, some 20,000 vehicles being made in 1928 and 1929. Later GMC started producing Buick engines specifically for its trucks with the bore and stroke altered to make them more suitable for use in commercial vehicles. These engines which were offered in different displacements would have production runs for more than twenty years.

Studebaker pickup truck production had not been resumed until 1927 when a new truck model was announced and subsequently produced until 1931 when the company again abandoned the production of trucks. In 1929 sales of International Harvester trucks had grown to approximately 50,000 and overall the public demand for pickup trucks was still growing.

The later years of the twenties also saw the development of a new phenomenon, that of the suburb. The growing availability of motor vehicles meant that people were now able to work in a city and commute in from its edges. This would gradually bring about a major shift in many aspects of life despite the oncoming depression.

Below: *By 1929 Ford trucks were available in colors other than black. One color on offer was L'Anse dark green, a shade specific to Ford.*

1925 Model TT Ford

This Model TT one-ton truck number 13,290,322 was built in 1925 and sold by the Vandemower-Taylor Motor Company of Denver to wheat farmer Clyde E. Jones of Nunn, Colorado whose name appeared on the title on March 11, 1926. It was supplied as a chassis cab and Jones had the six quarter lumer load bed built for carrying wheat. The truck has spent more than 70 years within 10 miles of Clyde Jones' farm and is now treasured by another farmer in Nunn, Dick Barnes.

Specifications

Owner: Dick Barnes
City: Nunn, Colorado
Make: Ford
Model: Model TT one-ton closed-cab truck
Year: 1925
Wheelbase: 124 inches

ENGINE
Model: In-line, four cylinder L-head
Capacity: 176.7 cubic inch
Ignition: Magneto

TRANSMISSION
Type: Manual

SUSPENSION
Front: Transverse, leaf spring, beam axle
Rear: Transverse, leaf spring, beam axle

BRAKES
Front: None
Rear: Twelve inch drums

WHEELS
Wooden spoked

TIRES
Front: 30x3 inch
Rear: 30x5 inch heavy service

PAINT & FINISH
Paint: 1925 Ford
Color: Black

Above: *From the left, Floyd Dahl, Leon Sandidge and Babe with the 1933 Ford V8 chassis cab that Floyd restored from the ground up with Leon's help. The load bed is made from teak and intended for hauling beet.*

Limp flags in the afternoon sun. Today's Bargain. '29 Ford pickup, runs good.
What do you want for fifty bucks – a Zephyr?

THE GRAPES OF WRATH. JOHN STEINBECK (1939).

MASS PRODUCTION

FORD AND CHEVROLET slugged it out through the Great Depression even as overall industry production totals of automobiles dropped. Chevrolet introduced an in-line six cylinder engine and Chevrolet sales soared to the extent that they were outselling Fords. Ford retaliated with a V8 in 1932, the year total production approximated 1.3 million vehicles and America elected its first woman senator. Hattie Caraway, a Democrat, was elected to represent Arkansas. New for 1932 was the Model B Ford, subsequently to be nicknamed "The Deuce" which, despite being launched during the Depression, became one of the most famous of thirties' American cars. One of the main reasons for its popularity was that it came with an L-head V8 engine, although a flathead four was an option. The V8 endowed The Deuce with considerable performance which would subsequently make it a favorite among the hot rod fraternity. It has been said by hot rodders that The Deuce is one of the few vehicles that looks as good with its curved fenders fitted as with them stacked against the garage wall.

The V8 powered truck variant was the Model BB which also appeared in 1932. V8 engines were not new and were already in use in luxury cars such as the Lincolns, built by Ford but they were not available in mass produced cars and trucks.

The difficulty in manufacturing a mass-produced, and therefore cheap, V8 was in casting the crankcase block and cylinder banks as one unit. Up until 1932 the V8 was cast in three parts which had to be machined and fitted together. Against a background of the Depression the auto industry was suffering, even Ford had closed a number of his autoplants and laid off approximately 75,000 workers as his financial resources were over stretched. His pattern makers and foundrymen were working day and night to produce the complex V8 blocks, struggling to control 54 separate sand cores. The scrap rate was as high as 100% at times but eventually the casting problem was solved so that the affordable V8 became a reality. Of this breakthrough Henry Ford was able to say, "The V8 is the coming car for the majority of American drivers. As always, we have done the pioneer work. It will only be a short time until motor manufacturing practice will follow the trail we have blazed".

The design of the new Ford range progressed under Edsel Ford and designer Joe Galamb while engineer Gene Farkas redesigned the chassis in a way that eliminated the need for splash aprons between the body and running boards (one of the reasons it looks good without fenders.) When the 1932 Ford range went on sale, it consisted of ten car variants and four trucks. The latter vehicles were a sedan delivery, a Murray and Baker-Raulang bodied station wagon and two pickups. The pickups were a Murray bodied open cab and a closed cab truck. The sedan delivery (with a single side hung door rather than a pair, no back windows and no back seats as in a panel truck,) the Station Wagon Woody, and open cab pickup were built in small numbers, production totalled only 2,371 for all three but 14,259 of the closed cab pickups rolled off the Detroit line. Most of these vehicles were four cylinder powered because the V8 was not available for them until late in the model year.

The Murray-bodied open cab pickup was assembled from parts of other Fords including Model A leftovers but the closed cab pickup featured a new all-steel body that shared styling and parts with the cars. Although sales of the 1932 models were slow, mainly

Below: *The wheels of the restored 1933 Ford were painted 1975 Toyota yellow, the closest match to the original. The wheels were fitted with vintage style Country Squire tires.*

as a result of the Depression and Ford lost $75 million, the new engine re-established Ford as the leading automaker.

The depths of the Depression were plumbed in 1933 as thousands of the dust bowl farmers of Oklahoma and the surrounding regions drove west in search of a better life. Ford's range for the 1933-34 sales season included sedan deliveries that followed the lines of the redesigned car range while the Roadster and closed cab pickup models remained more like the 1932 range in appearance. Ford managed to stay ahead of Chevrolet in numbers of trucks sold despite Chevrolet's significant advances through the thirties. In 1930 for example, hydraulic shock absorbers, vacuum windshield wipers, electric fuel gauges and external rear view mirrors all became standard equipment in Chevrolet trucks. Chevrolet acquired a specialist truck body maker - Martin Parry Corporation - in the same year which led to the company offering a range of half-ton pickups, panel trucks

Below: *Built for hard work, not drag strips, this '33 Ford chassis cab was equipped however with the optional V8, the V8 that endeared itself to hot rodders across the US.*

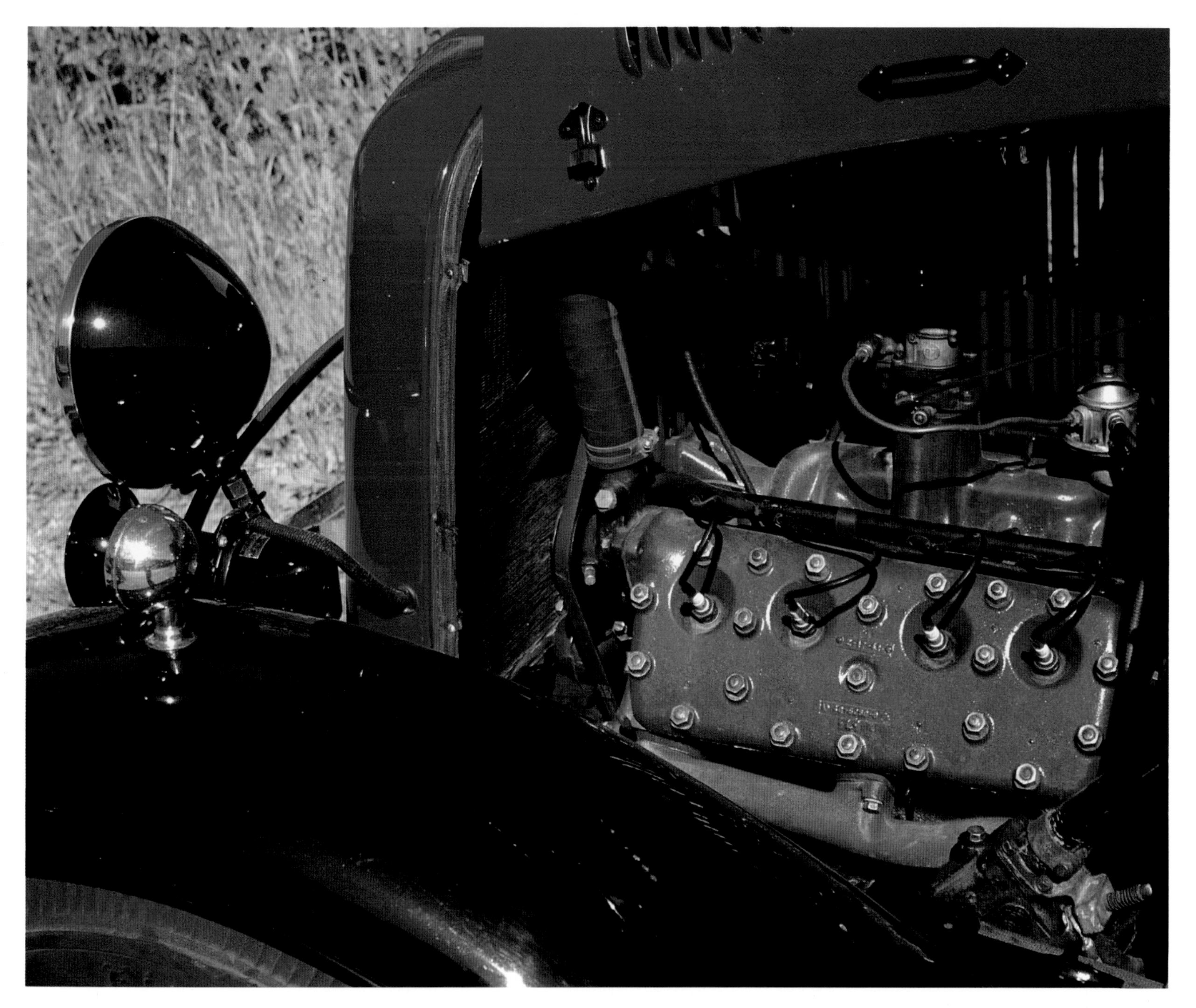

Above: *It is hard to imagine who could buy a new pickup in the early thirties as the Depression worsened. Despite this, Ford did announce the V8 in 1932.*

and canopy express trucks as factory models. The acquisition of Martin Parry would boost Chevrolet's sales in the light truck market far beyond the 32.7% sales share it had already achieved by this time. Through the thirties Chevrolet offered a range of colors, a synchromesh transmission and pushed its trucks hard through fleet sales. These improvements contributed to the company's market share climbing from that achieved in 1930 to 50% in 1933, the same year as it produced its millionth truck.

As the thirties moved on Chevrolet trucks became more streamlined and styled in the manner of its passenger cars, certain models shared the same front end sheetmetal. The range included larger capacity trucks including three-quarter and one-ton models. Progress continued and in 1934 Chevrolet trucks came equipped with hydraulic brakes – referred to in the slang of the time as "juice-binders" – and the cabs were built with one-piece steel roofs. This year saw the overall total number of trucks produced increase slightly over 1933. A range of trucks completely designed by Chrysler appeared in 1933. The new range included an in-line six cylinder engine, a feature that would endure until the sixties. The styling of the

Right: *Attention to detail is everywhere in this truck restoration, the driver's side spotlight mounted just below the windshield is a period accessory that was available between 1929 and 1935.*

line became distinctly car-like in appearance.

During the thirties IHC used alphabetical designations for its trucks, the A series was manufactured between 1930 and 1932, the C series from 1933 to 1934 and so on. There was no Series B, presumably because Ford was already using a similar designation at that time. Of these trucks the AW-1, for example, was a conventional three-quarter-ton truck powered by a four cylinder engine and available in chassis, panel, pickup, canopy truck, screen-side or sedan delivery configurations. The later Model C series for 1935 included the C-1, C-10, C-20 and M-3. The C-1 models were the half ton line in both 113- and 125 inch wheelbases. The C-10 models were three-quarter-ton trucks on a 133 inch wheelbase. The C-20 were larger trucks based on a 157 inch wheelbase and a maximum capacity of around 1.5 tons. The M-3 was a 133 inch wheelbase one-ton truck. It was during the

Left: *Larry Sterkel's 1935 Ford closed cab pickup street rod was rebuilt from the ground up. It is fitted with a modern Ford V8 and autobox and finished in Porsche Red.*

Far Left: *One of the most important aspects of building a street rod is getting it to sit just right. Notice how neatly the wheel and radial tire fit under the front fender.*

thirties that GMC really started mass production of a range of light trucks. The early thirties models had styling comparable with Fords of the day, the cabs had vertical windshields while the hoods were long and had louvered sides. The range for 1932 included the T-11 half-ton, T-15 three quarter-ton, T-15AA and T-17A one-ton models.

In 1935 the UAW (United Auto Workers) Union was formed and affiliated to the Congress of Industrial Organisations (CIO). The Chevy truck range for this year included Model EC and EA sedan deliveries, EB Suburban and various EB pickups. For 1936 Chevrolet would add a coupe delivery to the range, based on the FC series of passenger cars. A redesigned Ford range appeared in 1935, the year that Fords were the best selling cars and trucks in the US. The restyle incorporated a new narrower grille, a longer hood and more rounded fenders. This design was only slightly revised for 1936 with minor changes to the wheels and radiator grille shell. An unusual Ford truck appeared in 1937, it was a standard coupe car with a pickup body introduced to compete with Chevrolet's Coupe Delivery of the year before. The type was a poor seller for both companies and Ford

Below: *In the thirties Ford also offered larger payload versions of its pickups that used the same sheetmetal as the half tons but heavier axle and chassis components.*

Right: *Chevrolet's thirties trucks were not dissimilar to those made by Ford as the styling of this 1934 half-ton Model DB closed cab pickup demonstrates.*

discontinued its version at the end of that same model year although Chevrolet persevered with its version until the outbreak of World War Two. Plymouth commercial vehicles were offered between 1935 and 1942 alongside Dodge trucks as both companies were part of the Chrysler group. Plymouth was the low cost brand and dealers with joint Chrysler – Dodge franchises were offered an opportunity to increase their sales.

The first trucks from the Plymouth company were "commercial cars," with a sedan delivery, that is, having a car front end and a commercial back end. Production was numerically small but considered sufficiently worthwhile by the company for it to increase the range from 1938 onward. For 1939 the range included the PT81 pickup powered by an in-line six cylinder engine and equipped with a three speed transmission. In excess of 6,000 of these trucks were produced. By 1940 the company was offering the PT105 pickup truck which closely resembled the Dodge trucks of the time. It was powered by an in-line six cylinder engine of 201.3 cubic inch displacement that produced 79 bhp at 3,000 rpm. The truck was based on a 116 inch wheelbase chassis. The slightly upgraded models for 1941 became the PT125 series and these prewar models were to be the last trucks from Plymouth for thirty three years.

The GMC truck range was redesigned for 1936 and again for 1937, the T-14 of 1937 was a half-ton truck powered by a 230 cubic inch displacement in-line six cylinder engine. The front end featured a vertical grille with bullet shaped headlights positioned between the fenders and the sides of the hood while the remainder of the truck was of a basic configuration that would endure for several years. The T-16L was a three-quarter-ton version of the same model and the FL-16 was a walk-in delivery van version. In 1937 almost 35,000 GMC trucks were registered and the company offered a similar range for 1938 although the headlights were then mounted on the sides of the hood.

In 1937 Studebaker introduced a truck and San Francisco's Golden Gate bridge was opened to traffic. Studebaker sales were good and the company would remain in the pickup business until the closure of its Indiana plant in 1963. Its 1937 model was the Coupe Express which sourced most of its front sheetmetal from the, surprisingly named, Studebaker 5A Dictator car of the same year. This truck was based around a 116 inch wheelbase and power came from an in-line six cylinder L-head engine of 217.8 cubic inch displacement. For 1938 the pickup was also based on the concurrently produced car and again featured the same front end sheetmetal. Specialist machines were also offered and included large capacity furniture

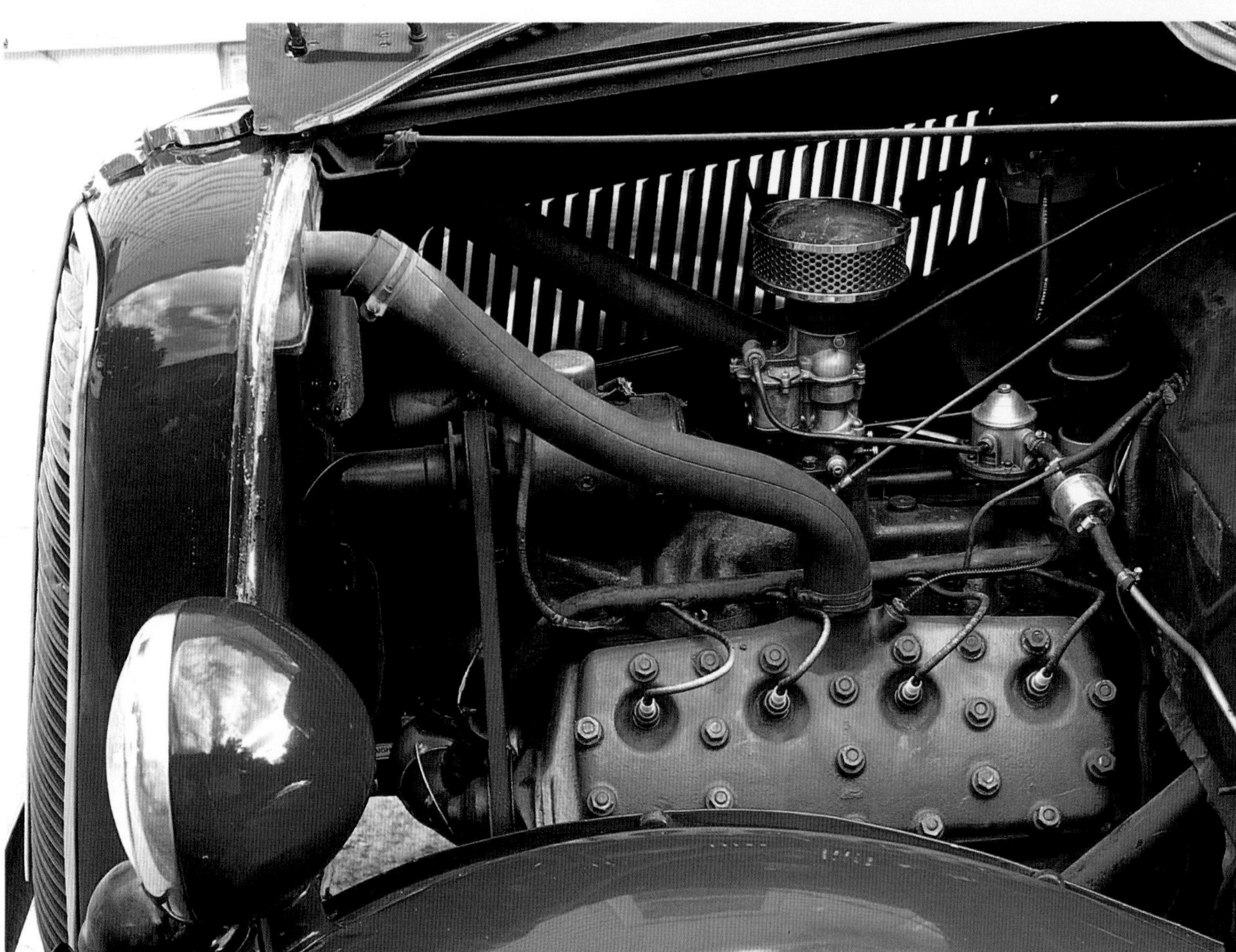

Above: *Ford's stylized V8 logo was incorporated into a number of the pickup's panels and other parts including the hubcaps and the bakelite horn push pictured here.*

Left: *The 1937 Ford half-ton pickups were offered with an L-head 136 cu in displacement V8 as standard but a larger capacity L-head V8 was an option.*

vans and fire trucks. In 1939, the pickup was to share its front end with Studebaker's redesigned car line.

IHC had expanded its truck line in 1936 to include seven basic truck models within its range. They all had styling similar to the 1935 models. This included a tall V-shaped grille, long hood with louvered sides, a tall cab and curved fenders that ran back to join the running boards. The smaller displacement trucks used Waukesha four cylinder engines while the larger models used an in-line six. A redesigned line of IHC trucks – the D-series – debuted in the spring of 1937. The appearance of the new models was considerably different as a result of redesigned grilles, two piece windshields and a fat-fendered appearance. The all-steel cab styling was referred to as 'turret-top styling' by its maker. This new range helped IHC increase its lead over Dodge and retain the third position in sales in the US with 30.22% of

Below: *Julian Guzman from Greeley, Colorado owns this 1937 Ford Model 77 half-ton Series 830 pickup. The 77 designation identifies it as the 85 hp version.*

the total truck market. The figure would drop considerably to only 10.24% for 1938 but surprisingly still leave IHC in third position. The IHC trucks continued almost unchanged for 1939 and IHC sales improved slightly to give the company 11.38% of the total US market.

Circumstances changed significantly again at Ford in 1938 when its trucks came assembled with a chassis that conformed to the specifications of the Society of Automotive Engineers' (SAE) recommendations which included both better brakes and larger diameter wheels. For 1938 Ford had also offered a range of one-ton trucks to complement its existing half-ton line. Matters continued to improve and by 1939 Ford trucks were equipped with "juice binders." The range had also been expanded to make it even more comprehensive with the addition of three-quarter-ton models. These trucks featured a rounded radiator grille shell, even more rounded fenders and steel wheels instead of the laced wire items used until this time.

GMC was aware of the changing trends and its range was redesigned for 1939. The windshields of the vehicles became two-piece and although the grille remained vertical it was redesigned to incorporate heavier looking horizontal inserts. The company offered four six-cylinder powered, half-ton models on a 113.5 inch wheelbase and three similarly engined models with a 123.75 inch wheelbase. The half-ton models were designated the Series AC-100 and AC-102 trucks while the greater payload models were the AC-150, AC-250 and ACL-300. In the various capacities there were chassis, chassis cab, pickup and panel truck models and in the larger capacity trucks there

Right: *Charwon Walter in his 1938 Chevrolet Model HD three-quarter-ton truck near his home in Windsor, Colorado. The truck has been in his family for forty years.*

Left: *Ford was justifiably proud of its V8 engines and the V8 logo can be found no less than ten times on this truck. The emblem is shown here on top of the radiator grille.*

96B97
COLORADO

COLLECTOR'S SERIES
96B97
COLORADO

Below: *These optimistic 1939 sales brochures are a reminder of a point in time when the world was heading inexorably toward war and soon Dodge would be building trucks for the US army.*

Left: *Trucks age like an old pair of Levis; the fading paint and each dent is testament to a lifetime of hard work, hard winters and hot summer sun.*

were also platform, stake bed and express models. This range was developed for the 1940 model year and walk-in delivery trucks of a forward control design (that is, where the driver sits over or forward of the front axle) were added to the existing range available.

Responding to world events in late 1939 Ford of Canada was conscripted into the British war effort to build a range of military vehicles as Hitler's German Armies had invaded Poland on September 1 1939. Canada joined the war in support of Great Britain who had declared war on Germany on September 3 1939. With an eye to quickly moving world affairs President Roosevelt declared a "limited emergency" within a week of the beginning of war in Europe and permitted further recruiting to both the US Army and The National Guard. The process had actually started earlier that summer when the strength of the army had been increased from 175,000 to 210,000 men. General Marshall, recently appointed Chief of Staff, established several tactical corps HQs with enough troops to create a fully functioning field army. He also reorganised the basic infantry divisions into five three-regiment "triangular" Divisions and aimed to make them both more maneuverable and flexible. In 1940 the first Corps maneuvers held since 1918 took place and these were later followed by Corps-v-Corps exercises.

While mechanization of the US Army had commenced in 1936 it had been a slow process because of a lack of funds. The coming war would irrevocably change the entire world in the years ahead, especially the methods of industrial mass production and automobile design.

FEB
9D 07

1933 Model B18 Ford

Despite the worst of the Depression, in 1933 in South Dakota someone purchased a new Ford chassis cab. The truck's original use is not recorded. The current owner, Floyd Dahl, has owned it for more than twenty years and Floyd carried out most of the restoration himself. Being a chassis cab model Floyd had to find and fit a rear body. A beet box from a similar vintage Chevy proved ideal, and it was the right size and exactly the sort of specialist rear body that would have been fitted to trucks like this.

Specifications

Owner: Floyd Dahl
City: Belle Fourche, South Dakota
Make: Ford
Model: Model B18 Chassis Cab Pickup
Year: 1933
Wheelbase: 106.5 inches

ENGINE
Model: L-head V8
Capacity: 221 cubic inch
Ignition: Coil and points

TRANSMISSION
Type: Three speed manual

SUSPENSION
Front: Transverse, leaf sprung beam axle
Rear: Leaf sprung, beam axle

BRAKES
Front: Drum
Rear: Drum

WHEELS
Laced

TIRES
Front: 6.00 x 16
Rear: 6.00 x 16
Country Squire

PAINT & FINISH
Paint: Owner
Color: 1970 Austin Healey red

Above: *The 1940 Ford half-ton pickup is acknowledged to be one of the best looking trucks ever built. This example is Bob Crouch's street rod which has been subtly altered to incorporate the gas filler flap in the rear fender and fitted with Halibrand mag wheels.*

Commander Cunningham soon appeared in the civilian pickup truck that he used for a staff car. The pilot and co-pilot, Ensigns James J. Murphy and H. P. Ady, were wide-eyed with surprise as Cunningham drove them to his command post. It was obvious that they had not known how heavily Wake had been bombed.

WAKE ISLAND. DUANE SCHULTZ (1978).

A TIME OF WAR

FORD BECAME UNIONIZED on June 21 1940 but this continuing development in industrial relations was generally overshadowed by world events. The war raged in Europe and America was initially an uneasy bystander. In 1940 expenditure was allocated to enable the US Army to procure much needed motor transport. This was due in part to the fact that the earlier reorganization of the army intended that non-divisional cavalry in the form of cavalry recon squadrons would ride "point" ahead of the new divisions. Each squadron would consist of three recon troops and nine recon platoons that would be transported in a defined number of White and Dodge trucks, Scout and Command cars respectively as well as motorcycles. For the civilian market, new for 1940 was the "Forty Ford" range which is generally acknowledged as featuring some of Ford's most distinctive trucks ever. The new trucks featured styling similar to the Ford cars for that year with a graceful hood that extended forward to finish almost in a point. The rear sheetmetal varied, depending on the type of vehicle, in a range that included panel truck, pickup and stake bed trucks. There were half-, three quarter- and one-ton variants which had 112, 122 and 122 inch wheelbases respectively. The Marmon-

Herrington 4x4 conversion for Ford's three-quarter-ton Model 11D Pickup was an innovation. Willys Overland was producing similarly styled trucks with hoods that, like Ford's, finished in a point. The Willys trucks had progressed from a flat grille with the introduction of the Model 77 in 1937. This became the Model 38 in 1939 and the Model 441 in 1940. In the latter year the company produced a total of 32,930 cars, trucks and Jeeps.

IHC introduced its Model K truck during the fall of 1940 for the 1941 model year. The styling was modern and incorporated integral fenders that also housed the headlights and a small vertical grille and a rounded hood. The new series was powered by the "green diamond" in-line six cylinder engine. With only minor changes this design would take IHC up to the outbreak of war. A new line of Studebaker pickups was introduced for the 1941 model year and designated the M series. The series used a common cab and front end sheetmetal that was unique to the truck line. The truck was built with economic priorities in mind and the running boards were interchangeable from side to side to minimize production costs. The front and rear fenders were interchangeable on a given side for the same reason. An I-beam front suspension system was used on the 113 inch wheelbase truck that was powered by an in-line six cylinder engine. The company sold more than 8,000 M-series trucks in its first year of production.

The Japanese air strikes against Pearl Harbor on Hawaii, Guam and the Philippines on December 7 1941 pushed America into World War Two. The US entered the war by Act of Congress the day after the airstrikes. Within days the United States Marine Corps was fighting to hold Wake Island. The Marines' determined stand for sixteen days against overwhelming odds was the first sign, soon after the disaster at Pearl Harbor, that although the road to victory would be long and costly, America would ultimately win.

In the final years before American involvement in World War Two the GMC trucks were redesigned again and most of them were redesignated as CC Series trucks. The redesign moved the headlights out onto the fenders, saw a new horizontal barred grille fitted and incorporated the sidelights into the tops of the headlight cowls. The styling remained unchanged on 1942 models until production was suspended for the duration of the war. The outbreak of World War

Left: *The 1940s Fords featured a pointed hood and grille which incorporated a V8 hood ornament. Truck styling was almost identical to that of Ford's car line.*

Two saw White move to Scout Car production and Dodge produce a range of military vehicles. The latter's vehicles included a three-quarter-ton 4x4 chassis which served as the basis for weapons carriers, ambulances and command cars. This vehicle was to be such a success that a postwar version of it known as the Power Wagon was introduced for the civilian market.

The other truck makers also assisted in the war effort. During the conflict IHC manufactured a range of machinery, including half-track vehicles, for the Allied armies. The company produced more than 13,000 International M-5 half tracks at its Springfield plant and also made a number of "Essential Use" pickups for civilians who required transport in order to assist the war effort. Willys Overland received a truck manufacturing stop order from the War Production Board on March 4 1942 and completely turned its attention to the quarter-ton 4x4 Jeep MB. Ford's civilian trucks were redesigned again for 1942 but then the company turned its efforts to winning World War Two. One of Ford's major contributions to the Allied cause was to turn some of its production capability over to building Willys MB Jeeps because Willys did not have the vast production capacity required. The

Below: *This street rod interior includes a late-model tilt column and a modern dashboard. Owner Bob Crouch built the street rod in Longmont, Colorado.*

Right: *The styling of the Ford truck was innovative at the time of its introduction. Notable in 1940 were the headlights in the fenders and their egg-shaped chrome trims.*

Far Right: *The rear fenders have been fitted with 1940 Ford passenger car tailgates. The truck is powered by a V8 and painted in Ford Regatta Blue.*

Ford-assembled Jeeps were designated Ford GPW and the company also produced an amphibious variant of the same vehicle which was designated the GPA. When the war ended Willys had built 358,489 MB Jeeps and Ford had built 277,896 of its equivalent, the GPW. The Ford Model GC was a military specification 4x4 pickup truck.

At Chevrolet, civilian truck production ended in January 1942 although the company later obtained permission to build a number of trucks. These were built to 1942 specifications and intended for high priority civilian use, until civilian trucks could start rolling off the Chevrolet lines again. It was 1944 before this could happen in large numbers. The numerous trucks produced for the Allied cause during World War Two meant that Chevrolet was the main supplier of 1.5 ton 4x4 trucks to the US Army for the duration of the conflict. The trucks were of a standardized design powered by a six cylinder in-line

gas engine, driving through a four speed transmission and two speed transfer case. The chassis was of a steel ladder type with leaf sprung suspension, a steel closed cab of a conventional design and a cargo rear body with a canvas tilt completed this, the NJ-G-7107. All Chevrolet plants participated in the war effort with the exception of Saginaw which exclusively made spares for the civilian Chevrolets already on the road. Chevrolet of Canada also produced numerous trucks for the Allies including the C30 and the 1311X3. In addition to other vehicles, GMC produced a vast number of the famous 6x6 "deuce and a half" 2.5 ton trucks for the Allied armies. These trucks were available in soft and hard cab models with a cab not dissimilar in design to that of the CC Series half-ton trucks. Studebaker assembled approximately 200,000 2.5 ton US6 6x4 and 6x6 trucks. Approximately half of these went to the USSR as Lend Lease equipment. The GAZ plant in Gorky, Russia produced a close copy of this truck in the postwar years. Studebaker also produced Wright Cyclone Flying Fortress engines and in excess of 15,000 Weasels. This was a light, fully-tracked military vehicle that was designed by Studebaker's engineers. Studebaker was another of the manufacturers permitted to produce a number of trucks for essential civilian use toward the end of the war. Chrysler made Sherman tanks while Pontiac made anti-aircraft guns.

Above: *Many Dodge Weapons Carriers were built during World War Two. This is a 1944 WC51, of the 2nd Armored Division 81st Reconnaissance Battalion.*

Right: *The three-quarter-ton Dodge WC-series vehicles were powered by an in-line six cylinder side valve engine.*

Above: *The interior of the Dodge WC51 was austere although the dashboard incorporated a speedo, ammeter, water temperature, fuel and oil pressure gauges.*

The war had an enormous impact on the truck manufacturers just as it had on every other aspect of life. For most of the major manufacturers 1946-48 model trucks were essentially nothing more than slightly improved pre-war machines. For their immediate postwar trucks, Ford retained the design features of the last prewar models including the so-called "Waterfall" grille, so called because it was composed of a row of vertical bars. In 1946 GMC resumed civilian production with light trucks that were also almost identical to their prewar models in order to give its staff time to design a new series of light trucks. IHC also resumed civilian production fully in 1946 when it reintroduced the K-series. These trucks were redesignated the KB-series with their redesign for 1947. Little had changed from the prewar models and little would change until 1950. Following the cessation of hostilities Studebaker reintroduced its prewar M-series trucks as 1946 and subsequently 1947 and 1948 models. As a result of the experience gained in wartime mass-production the company produced more than 67,000 trucks in 1947, a figure which

Right: *After the war Dodge turned its experience of building military vehicles into the creation of a hardworking civilian truck known as the Power Wagon.*

exceeded the total of all the trucks the company had produced prewar. Chevrolet produced numerous variations of its 1942-type trucks from 1944 to 1945 and then in a slightly revised form in 1946. The Dodge Power Wagon was a civilian version of the wartime WC-series and the model name was to be used on a variety of pickups from then on. Sales of Dodge trucks in this period were interesting; the years 1946 and 1947 were spectacular but there were drops in 1950 and 1953. Despite these dips, it was a time of increasing sales but the 1947 figures would not be surpassed until 1968 because of the sales decline of the late fifties. The company's market share fell to an all time low in 1961 before the beginning of an upward trend.

The new postwar GMC models were the FC series which featured GMC's all new "Advance Design" styling. The overall appearance was smooth and rounded. The grille was composed of a series of horizontal bars and a GMC logo was positioned on the hood above the grille. The headlights were mounted in the fenders enhancing the streamlined appearance. Underneath, the front suspension had been redesigned. Because the new truck had been introduced part way through 1947 it continued to be marketed through 1948. This design was retained for 1949 with only minor improvements like the repositioning of the gas tank. The half-ton FC-101 models were based on a 116 inch wheelbase and a line that

Right: *The 1946 Dodge WC-series half-ton pickup was almost identical to the models being built until civilian truck production was halted on April 30 1942.*

included chassis, chassis cab, pickup, panel truck, canopy express and suburban models. The FC-102 models were also rated at a half-ton but based on a chassis with a 125.25 inch wheelbase. Also on this chassis were the three-quarter-ton FC-152 models. Both FC-102 and FC-152 models were available as chassis, chassis cab, pickup and stakebed models. For 1950 matters continued in the same vein although some options changed and the horsepower of the 228 cubic inch in-line six cylinder engine was boosted.

Chevrolet trucks were fully redesigned for 1947 – they were described by Chevrolet as the Advance-Design – and now incorporated rear-hinged hoods in a redesigned cab with such innovations as a column gear shift. Sales generally boomed in the postwar years; 260,000 trucks made by Chevrolet were sold in 1947. The new 1947 design was sequentially upgraded with vented windows, new door latches, a redesigned grille and new autobox being introduced in 1951, 1952 and 1954. During this period Chevrolet offered half-, three-quarter- and one-ton pickups on 116, 125.25 and 137 inch wheelbases respectively. In each capacity class they offered pickups in the following configurations, chassis, chassis cab, pickup, platform and stake bed. In addition there were half- and one-ton panel trucks and canopy wagons. The three series trucks were designated 3100, 3600 and 3800 increasing with payload and wheelbase. These numerical designa-

Above left: *Dodge, like other US automakers, brought back civilian prewar trucks in the immediate postwar years to give its designers and engineers time to design new models.*

DODGE
DODGE
TENNESSEE
GSK 978
Volunteer State

tions continued for 1948, 1949 and into the fifties. While the overall appearance of the various models remained the same there were minor upgrades and increasing numbers of options as one model year succeeded another. In 1950 the extra-cost options included rear view mirrors, color combinations, leather seats, chrome radiator grille, deluxe equipment, double acting shock absorbers front and rear, spare wheel and tire carrier, heavy duty radiator, dual tail lights, heavy duty rear springs, a school bus chassis, an oil bath aircleaner, heavy duty clutch, four speed transmission, engine speed governor (to control the speed) and numerous tire options.

Ford's first new postwar range of trucks made the news in 1948. It was the introduction of the F-series of trucks that ranged from the half-ton F-1 to the three ton F-8. The F-series has, of course, endured for more than fifty years. For 1948 the styling had been altered radically from the previous models. The headlights

Left: *The 1946 Dodge on the road. This truck was one of 96,490 Dodges sold in that year, a figure which pushed Dodge into third place in terms of truck sales.*

Far left: *The curved fenders seen on this 1946 model lasted on Dodge trucks until the complete redesign of the half-ton models that was unveiled for the 1948 model trucks.*

were now set into the recessed, horizontally barred grille and the fenders were squared off and joined across the top of the radiator grille below the hood. The cab was larger in every dimension than before and rubber mounted to the chassis. The new half-ton truck was known as the F-1 and also available as the F-2 and F-3 as a three-quarter-tonner. The basic style endured through 1952 although the grille was considerably redesigned for 1951. The all new postwar Dodges also appeared in 1948 identified as the Series B models. The B-1-B was a half-ton, the B-1-C was a three-quarter-ton and the B-1-D was a one-ton. The company made a number of upgrades and options available through the fifties including automatic transmissions, column gear shifts, grilles, instrument panels as well as upgraded cab styling and a variation on the cargo box.

A new line of Studebaker trucks appeared in 1949 namely the 2R series. In the range were half-ton 2R5 models, three-quarter-ton 2R10 models and one-ton 2R15 models. These trucks were of a completely new design, drawn by Robert Bourke and shared no sheetmetal with Studebaker's concurrent car range. The 2R5 and 2R10 models used 112 and 122 inch wheelbases respectively and were powered by in-line six cylinder engines. The trucks were assembled in the wartime plant that Studebaker had used to assemble airplane engines. The plant had been built by the US

Below: *The Dodge WC half-ton truck was powered by an L-head, in-line six cylinder engine that displaced 217.7.76 cu in. It had a compression ratio of 6.6:1.*

Right: *One area where the prewar and postwar Dodge trucks did vary slightly was in the type and construction of seats fitted. The later ones were of an improved design.*

Left: *The Ford F-1 of 1948 was Ford's first all-new postwar truck and its styling ran on into 1949 when this truck that now belongs to Mike Yackey was manufactured.*

Above right: *This F-1 has clocked up more than 300,000 miles in its half century on Colorado's highways. It is almost as standard as the day it was made.*

Right: *A new dashboard incorporated all the instruments in one panel rather than as separate gauges, although the same engine functions were still monitored.*

government for the war production and after the war Studebaker bought it from the government and prepared it for truck production. The initial postwar sales boom did not last long and before the end of the decade the number of trucks moving off dealers' showroom floors had decreased. To combat this sales decline, Studebaker instituted a year model registration procedure that meant a 1949 built truck could be registered as a 1950. This system was similar to that already employed by IHC. The result was that the smaller manufacturers were no longer forced to compete with new lines from the bigger manufacturers each fall.

The mud on the battlefields and supply routes of World War Two had proven the extraordinary ability of four wheel drive vehicles beyond all doubt. In light truck terms Dodge and Willys had proven four wheel

Above: *The Ford F-1 was one model in a range of trucks offered by Ford. The longer F-2 rated as a three-quarter-ton model. This is a 1951 model.*

Right: *The types of load bed offered on F-1 and F-2 trucks varied. While this is a stake bed type, there were also chassis cabs, panel trucks and platform models.*

drive technology and saw the way to further increase the versatility of civilian trucks. Willys was among the first to see the advantages that four wheel drive would offer commercial vehicle users and so offered a range of four wheel drive pickups alongside its Jeeps. The styling of the trucks differed from that of the first civilian Jeeps but the design of their grille and front fenders left no doubt as to which company had produced them. The pickup trucks featured a steel closed cab with a variety of rear body types being available including a stepside, a stakebed and a chassis cab to allow the instalation of specialist equipment on the back. The pickup range was complemented by a line of panel trucks and an estate car line. The four wheel drive models were capable of having power take offs fitted to the gearbox to drive machinery. The first 4x4 truck made by Willys rolled off the Toledo, Ohio production line in February 1948 and trucks continued to do so until 1963 with only minor changes over the years. The grille was later redesigned and a one piece windshield substituted for the two piece item originally used. It wouldn't be until the fifties that the major US manufacturers would include 4x4 pickups in their regular lines.

USA 20284
FROM US PORT AGENCY
WAR SHIPPING ADM.NY
WEIGHT 5250 LBS
LENGHT 167 IN
WIDTH 83 IN
HEIGHT 85,50 IN
VOL 684 CU.FT.

1944 Dodge T214-WC51

In 1942 the range of US Army 4x4 half-ton vehicles that had been introduced in 1936 were superseded by a range of three-quarter-ton models. Dodge became the largest producer of this type and the weapons carrier was one of a range of command cars, carryalls and ambulances. While the ambulances were referred to as "meat wagons" the weapons carriers were often known as "beeps," an acronym for "big jeeps." These trucks were a common sight in the European and Pacific theaters of operations.

Specifications

Owner: Colin Ward
City: Tidworth, England
Make: Dodge
Model: WC51 Weapons Carrier
Year: 1944
Wheelbase: 98 inches

ENGINE
Model: In-line side-valve six cylinder
Capacity: 230.2 cubic inch
Ignition: Coil and points

TRANSMISSION
Type: Three speed manual. Single speed transfer box. Part time 4x4

SUSPENSION
Front: Leaf sprung beam axle
Rear: Leaf sprung beam axle

BRAKES
Front: Drum
Rear: Drum

WHEELS
Steel split rims

TIRES
Front: 9.00 x 16 Bargrips
Rear: 9.00 x 16 Bargrips

PAINT & FINISH
Paint: US Army
Color: Olive Drab/ US Army markings

Above: *Chevrolet introduced its first line of postwar trucks, the Advance-Design trucks in May 1947. The basic design ran for several years into the fifties with minor changes to trim and finish. This half-ton model belongs to Hillbilly Ray.*

'Optimo City is the blur of filling stations and motels; the brief congestion of mud-spattered pickup trucks that slows you down before you hit the open road once more'

J. B. JACKSON. THE ALMOST PERFECT TOWN (1952).

THE FABULOUS FIFTIES

IN JANUARY 1950 a completely new range of trucks - the L-Series - was unveiled by IHC. The trucks were both restyled and re-engineered and the styling now incorporated wide, flat fenders, a less rounded hood and significant changes to both the radiator grille and trim. Under the hood was a new in-line six cylinder overhead valve engine. This style ran until 1953 when it would be superseded by the R-series which was a development of the L-series. The front end was again redesigned and become concave with an oval aperture. A two-tone paintjob was an option as was a model with a greater payload. The standard half-ton pickup was known as the R-100 and had a 115 inch wheelbase while the R-102 was the heavier truck with the same wheelbase. The R-110 was the longer wheelbase variant also available as the R-111 and R-112. These trucks were to remain in production until 1955 when the S-series would make its debut. The 1949 2R truck was a good seller for Studebaker so few changes were made for 1950, 1951, 1952 or the final year of 2R production in 1953. At GMC it was a similar story for 1951, 1952, and 1953 as only minor changes were made leading up to the major redesign for 1955.

The Korean War had started on June 25 1950 when North Korean soldiers invaded South Korea by crossing the 38th Parallel, the line at which the country had been arbitrarily partitioned in 1945. In response to the outbreak of this war the US Department of Defense reactivated the Ordnance Tank Automotive Center in Detroit, Michigan to again mobilize the automotive industry for war production. On January 15 1951 Dodge began building trucks for a military contract for example. Dodge built a truck designated the M37 for the new military contracts. It was clearly a development of the WC series of World War Two and similarly styled but upgraded. Most of the automakers had received military contracts of one sort or another but in excess of 8 million cars, trucks, and buses were produced in the US in 1950, estimated to be more than 75% of all the vehicles made in the world that year.

The Korean War continued into 1951 as the People's Republic of China sent troops and assistance to the communist North Koreans. In order to avoid raising the stakes too high, President Truman was forced to sack General MacArthur, the UN Commander in Chief when he talked of invading China. This escalation led to restrictions on the amount of certain metals including zinc, chromium, tin, and nickel that could be used by the American auto industry for work other than that related to defense. Chrysler and Cadillac were making tanks and GMC truck plants were assembling the M-135 6x6 truck for the US Army. Numerous other restrictions came into force as a result of this latest conflict, the National Production Agency (NPA) limited both car and truck production in order to ensure a continuous flow of equipment for the war. The NPA assigned a quota of trucks to each manufacturer based on its percentage market share. Dodge's NPA quota, for example, was 13% of the industry total. The Korean War dragged on through 1952, the year that Republican Dwight D. Eisenhower was elected president, and ended only after the agreement at Panmunjon in July 1953. The cost had been high, including 51,000 American dead and the face of world politics had changed. The Korean War had been the first confrontation of the big powers in the nuclear

Right: *Alison Thomas owns this 1952 Dodge B-3-B pickup which is painted to look as if it belongs to a fifties' hot rod shop in Santa Maria, California, hence the whitewall tires.*

Below: *The dash of the 1952 Dodge had unusual cowls for the speedometer and radio speaker. The truck was powered by an in-line six of 217.8 cu in displacement.*

DODGE
Superior
SPEED SHOP
SANTA MARIA

age and was the model for the brinkmanship of numerous Cold War era conflicts to come.

The F-series trucks had carried Ford into the Fifties on a very firm footing and Ford became the nation's number two automaker, partially as a result of a serious labor dispute at Chrysler. The F-series underwent a redesign in 1951 when a redesigned grille was fitted. In 1952 two new overhead valve engines were made available, an in-line six and a V8. The major facelift however was saved for 1953 and Ford's Golden anniversary, with its most major redesign in two decades. Most significant from the truck buyer's point of view was that the F-series was given the three-digit designations that have been used ever since. The F-1 became the F-100, the F-2 and F-3 became the F-250, and the F-4, slightly downgraded, became the F-350. This seems straightforward but there were, with the numerous options, a total of 194

Below: *In 1955 Chevrolet introduced a stylized half-ton pickup as a limited edition. It was the Model 3124 Cameo Carrier and featured fiberglass slabsided rear fender sides.*

Right: *The 3124 Chevy was powered by a V8 as the front fender badges indicate. This one was perfectly restored from a rusty pickup by Lewis C. Helton in Colorado.*

models in the Ford truck range. The F-100, as the new model was officially known, or "Effie" as it soon became referred to, was introduced on March 13 1953 with a sleeker and more modern appearance than that which had gone before. It was available in a great number of variants of which the F-100s were the one -ton models available as platform, stake trucks, and stepsides. Straight six and V8 engines were available depending on customer preference. Larger capacity versions were the three-quarter-ton F-250 and F-350. Larger again was the F-500. The basic design would last several years with only minor upgrades in terms of grille changes, body panel variations, interior changes, and equally minor improvements.

Innovation in the form of factory 4x4s came from Ford in the fifties. These trucks were also introduced in response to suggestions emanating from Chevrolet about the company's own 4x4. International Harvester introduced its first 4x4 pickup in 1953 with the R-series. In late 1955 the company, then the third largest pickup truck manufacturer in the US, brought out the S-series of trucks including the 4x4 S-120 model. There were 13 variations of this truck with four different wheelbases, chassis cabs, stake beds and platform trucks. Ford, GMC and Chevrolet continued to offer 4x4 trucks, usually in the form of a four wheel drive variant of an existing truck. Ford's first contenders for a section of this growing market were the 1956 F-100 and F-250 4x4 models which were available as both pickups and chassis cabs. Prior to this, four wheel drive pickups from Ford had only been available as specialist conversions carried out by Armon Herrington, an established automotive engineering company and truck maker. Dodge built a serious 4x4 working truck during the fifties based on the military vehicles it had supplied to America's services

Above: *The 1955 Chevrolet Cameo was powered by an overhead valve V8 engine with a displacement of 265 cu in achieved through a bore and stroke of 3.75 x 3 in.*

during World War Two. It was known as the Power Wagon and was considered the undisputed king of the highway in America's backwoods. The Power Wagon was favoured for logging and oil exploration and on wilderness construction sites such as remote dam projects. Power Wagons were available with a variety of bodies and all were built by Chrysler's Dodge Truck Division and also briefly marketed under the De Soto and Fargo names. The Power Wagon later spawned a whole range of heavy duty 4x4s including the Chevrolet and GMC Suburbans and Crew Cabs.

The comprehensive nature of the new model range in 1953 represented a huge investment from the Ford Motor Company, therefore further changes were minimal until 1956 when Ford was forced to respond to Chevrolet's 1955 introduction of newly competitive products. Ford innovated in an area of vehicle design that was still up and coming, that of safety; tubeless tires, a safety steering wheel, better door locks and a shatterproof rear view mirror. Ironically these inexpensive upgrades failed as a sales incentive but only ten years later government regulations would force such measures on the US automotive industry. The all new GMC and Chevrolet ranges of 1955 model trucks were supposed to go on sale alongside the redesigned car line in the fall of 1954 but the scale of Chevrolet's model line revision, sales

Above: *Standard features on the Cameos were deluxe cab equipment and a special red three-spoked steering wheel. Cameos were finished in Bombay Ivory with red accents.*

pressures from Ford, and Korean War contracts forced the company to delay the introduction of the new line until April 1955. The first series of 1955 trucks were slightly upgraded 1954 models that were on sale from August 1954 until March 1955. In 1954 another event took place that would later affect America's future. This was the agreement which partitioned Vietnam into North and South and recognised both Cambodia and Laos as independent nations following the end of French rule.

The mid-fifties Federal program of Interstate and Freeway building within the US caused a shift in the buying patterns for trucks. Demand increased for higher performance trucks making the large displacement in-line six and V8 powered models ever more popular.

The first 1955 series of Chevrolet trucks incorporated two immediately apparent changes. These were to the grille and the windshield. The grille was changed from having a series of horizontal bars to a single heavier central bar and a single vertical bar, the Chevrolet logo was stamped into the horizontal bar. The windshield became a single piece item. The interior of the trucks was redesigned with a revised steering wheel and dash arrangement. Less obvious was the redesigned load bed for pickup variants that was lower at the sides but deeper overall. The three speed transmission was beefed up and a Hydra-Matic auto-

STUDEBAKER

Above: *The dashboard of the 1958 Transtar Deluxe. Studebaker offered many items as extra cost options on its range including ashtrays, extra sun visors and rear view mirrors.*

Left: *Steve Doerschlag rebuilt this custom 1958 Studebaker Transtar Deluxe with a hood and grille from a 1955 model. It has American Racing Equipment custom wheels.*

box was an option. The designations of 3100, 3600 and 3800 from the forties continued although some years earlier the 3700 had been added for the Dubl-Duty models.

The Chevy trucks that would become legendary however, were introduced as the second series redesign for 1955, albeit using the 3100 series designations. The new trucks featured wrap-around windshields, redesigned fenders and truck beds and had the option of a V8 engine. The 3100 was the half-ton commercial vehicle while the 3200 was a half-ton on a longer wheelbase, the 3600 was the three-quarter-ton and the 3800 the one-ton. The Dubl-Duty models used 3400, 3500, 3700 for its various versions. A Cameo pickup model appeared as a limited edition and the new design would endure with minor upgrades until the restyled model of 1958 was unveiled with its dual headlights.

Chevrolet had introduced the new models with what it described as "taskforce" styling that included new features such as the panoramic windshield that wrapped around the corners of the cab, the flatter hood, wing and roof line, as well as the egg-crate

Left: *As part of a minor redesign for 1955, Studebaker trucks powered by a V8 engine were fitted with a new hood ornament bearing the number 8.*

Right: *Colorado resident Steve Doerschlag also owns this two tone 1955 Studebaker truck which he has converted to a dualie (a truck with twin rear wheels) for use in connection with his work.*

grille. The trucks were only slightly upgraded for 1956 and would subsequently be upgraded again for 1957 in a similarly minor way.

The new GMC trucks were also considerably more angular than their predecessors. The front end featured a two bar grille reminiscent of passenger cars of the era and was complemented by hooded headlights and a massive chrome bumper. The GMC logo was mounted on the lower portion of the hood front in a stylized form. The cab was redesigned to incorporate a wraparound windshield and the higher front fender line ran right through the cab and doors. The new designs were designated as Series 100, 102, 150, 251, 252, 253 models reflecting wheelbases and payloads. The trucks fitted with the optional V8 were given an additional '8' suffix. In this way the half-ton model on a 114 inch wheelbase was a Model 100 while the V8 variant was the 100-8. The Series 150-8 trucks were three-quarter-ton trucks on a 123.25 inch wheelbase and V8 powered. Of these models, registrations for the 1955 calendar year totalled 84,877 vehicles.

The 1956 GMC models continued almost unchanged from the 1955 ones although the V8 models were no longer listed as a separate series, the V8 simply became an option. The engines were increased in displacement to 269.5 and 316.6 cubic inches for the six- and eight-cylinder units respectively. A redesigned grille was the only obvious styling change for 1957 but for 1958 the range was redesigned in several small ways and a pickup body made by Wide-

Below: *The owner of this Studebaker Transtar deluxe has increased the truck's performance by fitting a 1957 Golden Hawk sedan McCullough supercharger.*

STUDEBAKER

STEVE DOERSCHLAG
CUSTOM HOMES

Side steel was introduced. Less decorative hub caps, dual headlights and a new grille changed the exterior appearance.

During this period it was not just Ford, GMC and Chevrolet who were redesigning their trucks to tempt customers; Studebaker's range of trucks had been redesignated the 3R series for 1954 and given a minor facelift. Much of the sheetmetal was the same although the grille was redesigned and a curved one piece windshield superseded the two piece item used until then. For 1955 styling changes were kept to a minimum but numerous upgrades were made to the power train of the trucks. Because of these changes, including the use of an overhead valve V8 in some models, the trucks were again redesignated, this time as the E-series. There were E5 and E7 half-ton trucks and E10 and E12 three-quarter tonners, the E7 and E12 models were the V8 powered versions. The V8 models proved popular and helped Studebaker achieve a good sales total for the year.

In October 1954 Studebaker merged with Packard but it was not really to either company's advantage. Studebaker lost money for two years following the

Above: *The dashboard of Steve Doerschlag's 1950 Studebaker truck. The dash insert is in a contrasting color and matches that of the radiator grille.*

Left: *The Studebaker stakebed platform truck is a one-ton model. The increased payload was achieved through the use of heavier duty wheels and suspension.*

Left: *Ford redesigned the radiator grille in its F-100 Series trucks for 1956. The V-section of the single bar carried a V8 emblem on V8 trucks and was left plain on six cylinder ones.*

Right: *This 1956 F-100 was rebuilt by Bill Smith of Greeley, Colorado and is powered by a 390 cu in V8. The classic lines are enhanced by 1994 Lincoln Portofino Blue paint.*

merger. This meant that by 1956 the money was not available for a complete redesign of the truck range. A new name – Transtar – and a minor redesign was all that was done. Sales were not as good as hoped and Studebaker truck production was moved back to the main Studebaker plant and the wartime plant leased to another company. The Studebaker company began to make annual changes to its model line and alongside the Transtar introduced a basic pickup known as the Scotsman. It was the lowest priced pickup on sale in the US in 1958.

Below: *The frame up refurbishment of this truck took its owner nearly five years, in which time he mixed restoration and practicality to build a "driver" without losing the original feel.*

STEEL RADIAL
SX 1000 SR

The S-series of trucks was made by IHC from late 1955 until mid-1957. The design was apparently refined from the R-series although the trucks had a more square appearance partially as a result of the headlights being mounted high on the fenders rather than within the confines of the radiator grille. The windshield had been redesigned to increase visibility. Options of payloads continued and a variety of optional interiors were made available. At this time IHC held third position in terms of US sales and again announced new models in late 1957. The next major restyle from Dodge came in 1957 when the front end was restyled and the Sweptside D100 was introduced, larger capacity V8s – 315 cubic inches -

Above: *Ford also offered a panel truck variant of its F-100 half-ton trucks on the 110 inch wheelbase. This is the 1956 in-line six-powered version.*

Left: *A comparison of the 1956 F-100 half-ton truck with the F-600 from the same year's range. The cabs are identical but the larger payload model had 20 inch diameter wheels.*

were fitted and even the utilitarian Power Wagon was redesigned although the original style model was still available. The redesigned cabs featured a one-piece rear hinged hood and were changed slightly for the next year when double headlights were fitted.

IHC considered 1957 its 50th year in truck manufacture and brought out anniversary models to mark the occasion. The range of trucks which had been significantly redesigned were designated the A-series to denote the anniversary. The styling was modern and angular and the trucks came with a choice of bed styles – there was the custom pickup and the pickup which were effectively fleetside and stepside models respectively. The fleetside type bed was constructed using the rear fenders of the IHC Travelall station wagon. For 1959 the range of trucks was designated the B-series which was the previous year's A-series models with minor updates including quad headlights and a chrome car-like grille. This range was to be carried over into 1960 with the only major change being that a V8 engine was now standard equipment. Ford's next overall styling change was made in 1957 and in the same year the Ford Ranchero made its debut. This new truck combined car and truck features to offer a car-type cab and front sheetmetal with a pickup load bed between the rear fenders. Similar models continued through 1958 and 1959 although in the latter year the base model Ranchero was discon-

Above: *Becky Moreland's 1956 International Harvester S-120 truck in South Dakota. The S-120 designation indicates that this is a three -quarter-ton model.*

Right: *The Ford F-100 pickup was completely restyled for 1957, the year this two tone truck was built. The modern look was enhanced by flush fenders and sides.*

tinued leaving only the top of the range Custom Ranchero available.

The 1958 Chevrolet Apache used the same basic cab as the previous Chevrolet truck models but featured a redesigned hood, grille and fenders. The fenders incorporated double headlights and the trim was redesigned. The stepside bed continued although later in the year Chevrolet offered what it termed the Fleetside bed which was more like the smooth sides of the Cameo models but fabricated in steel. A four wheel drive transmission was available as an option. The basic styling continued until the new 1960 trucks were unveiled in the fall of 1959. As was usual the basic model was upgraded and offered with slightly different options each year. The El Camino was brand new for 1959 and was seen in many ways as a car and truck hybrid. It combined contemporary car front styling and a truck bed between the styled rear fenders. In this same year Chevrolet began to use the C10 - C30 model designations that are still in use.

The end of the fifties saw the sands of time shifting again; Sputnik, the world's first satellite had gone into orbit in 1957 so beginning the space age. In recognition of the fact that such new technology would no doubt have a place in the automobile indus-

LFO
274

try various manufacturers produced futuristic vehicles. GMC's truck and coach division rolled out the Turbo-Titan, an experimental truck designed and built to use a gas turbine engine for power. Ford produced the similarly experimental Glidaire which traveled on a cushion of air rather than wheels. The company took the idea a step further and followed the Glidaire with the Levacar which like the Curtiss-Wright Aircar was also an air-cushion vehicle. By 1959 Chevrolet, as part of GMC, produced the Turbo Titan II, a second gas turbine powered truck and Chrysler experimented with an electro-chemical source of power while Cadillac experimented with radar for cars. Also hinting at future developments was the fact that 1957 was the year that saw the first imported VW trucks and vans take to America's highways.

Left: *Barry Redman restored this 1957 one-ton four cylinder engined F4-134 4x4 pickup. It is of a design introduced by Willys Overland in the immediate postwar years.*

Far right: *The designers at Willys Overland combined the familiar flat-paneled appearance of the Jeep with the curves that were popular in the fifties as on this door handle.*

Right: *The interior of the truck is austere. It was equipped with a bench seat, a steering wheel with a Willys Overland logo in the horn push and extra gear levers.*

CHEVROLET

1959 Chevrolet Apache

In the fall of 1957 Chevrolet announced redesigned versions of its 1957 trucks for 1958. The changes included a redesigned grille, new trim and a shift to dual headlights. Changes were minimal for 1959. The Fleetside pickup body with a missile-shaped bulge along the exterior was made from steel and phased in to replace the Cameo models. The panoramic rear window seen here was an extra-cost option for 1959. A two-tone paint scheme and "custom cab" were also offered.

Specifications

Owner: Cool Cars Only
City: Longmont, Colorado
Make: Chevrolet
Model: Apache 3134
Year: 1959
Wheelbase: 114 inches

ENGINE
Model: In-line ohv six cylinder
Capacity: 235.5 cubic inch
Ignition: Coil and points

TRANSMISSION
Type: Three speed manual

SUSPENSION
Front: Leaf sprung beam axle
Rear: Leaf sprung beam axle

BRAKES
Front: Drum
Rear: Drum

WHEELS
15 inch steel rims

TIRES
Front: 6.70 x 15
Rear: 6.70 x 15
Country Squire

PAINT & FINISH
Paint: Chevrolet
Color: Tartan turquoise

Above: *Sixties trucks would feature bold, new styling as illustrated by this 1960 GMC which incorporated a concave design feature that ran along the fenders, doors, and truck bed.*

'Francesca heard the out-of-tune pickup go by. She lay there in bed, having slept naked for the first time in as far back as she could remember. She could imagine Kincaid, hair blowing in the wind curling through the truck window, one hand on the wheel, the other holding a Camel.'

THE BRIDGES OF MADISON COUNTY. ROBERT JAMES WALLER (1991).

THE SPACE AGE

As the sixties opened, the spaceship-style fins were still to be seen on the rear fenders of many American sedans and hints of similar styling appeared on trucks as the US accounted for almost 48% of worldwide automobile production. The results of a GMC redesign appeared in 1960 when the company's trucks were given a more modern looking cab that had a lower overall height than previously. A concave styling feature ran along the sides of the fenders, cab and bed. The full width hood had lights in pods on either side while the headlights were dual and mounted in the grille. The rear of the cab featured an overhang while the front included a wraparound windshield. Underneath the trucks were also a number of new features including a new front suspension system, a redesigned frame that was both stronger and lighter and an optional V6 engine of 305 cubic inch displacement. Four wheel drive was an option at $650 extra and three payloads of truck were available. The P1000 series were the half-ton models while the P1500 and P2500 were the three-quarter- and one-ton models respectively. The choice of body types across these ranges included chassis cab, pickup, stake bed, panel, wideside and fenderside models. As GMC did not produce trucks on a strict model-year by model-year basis the range did not necessarily change in the fall of each year, the 1960 trucks went forward into 1961 completely unchanged and only some styling changes were made for 1962. The hood was lowered and rounded off eliminating the vents in the leading edge and a single long vent was positioned between the parking lights. Other minor changes included a change of hub caps and redesigned badges. This redesign also carried GMC's trucks on through the 1963 model year.

On November 9 1960 the Democrat John F. Kennedy was elected President. The decade got off to a good start for Chevrolet when it became America's number one truck maker in 1961, albeit by the narrow margin of 3,670 trucks over Ford. Chevrolet's production was 30.39% of the market share. The C10 was one of a series of 185 trucks made by the company in 1960. Such a large number was achieved by the manufacture of a number of different wheelbases as well as a number of optional engines and transmissions. The K-prefix models were 4x4 variants of the C-series. The trucks had been redesigned to include a redesigned grille with repositioned headlights. The fenders, body sides and hood were redesigned with a sculpted line down either side of the body. The range

included the half-ton series 1000, the three-quarter-ton commercial and Dubl-Duti Series 2000 models and the one-ton Series 3000 models. Minor styling changes took the line into 1961 and a restyled hood took it forward into 1962. The styling changes were kept to a minimum for 1963 but a coil sprung front suspension arrangement was introduced at the same time on the 4x2 C-series trucks. In 1962 Chevrolet truck number 8 million was produced and the El Camino appeared as a mid-size pickup similar in configuration to the Chevelle automobile. Production at Chevrolet's plants was in full swing and a further million trucks had been produced by 1964.

The decade did not get off to such a good start for Studebaker. The last years of the fifties had been difficult ones for the company until it introduced the Lark passenger car which sold well and improved its financial situation considerably. There were no Lark-type pickup trucks but there were Lark panel trucks and the Larks later appeared on the Studebaker Champ

Above: *During the early sixties, trucks became more angular, as this 1962 Chevrolet demonstrates, but were no less flamboyant than their fifties predecessors.*

Right: *Pat Taylor from Greeley Colorado owns this 1962 Chevrolet pickup which has been fitted with custom alloy wheels and modern radial tires.*

06J40
COLORADO

Left: *Concave styling features were a feature of early sixties trucks and were incorporated into the front edge of the hood which also included the turn signals.*

pickups. The Champ and the Transtar went on sale in 1960 the Champ in both 4x2 and 4x4 models. Studebaker trucks were manufactured only until 1963.

The sixties were important years for Dodge who built a comprehensive line of pickups. The redesigned Dodge cabs were lower and wider than those which had gone before and mounted on new chassis with different wheelbases. Future revisions were minimal and included a switch from single to dual headlights and back again. In the range were Sweptline pickups, Sweptline Power Wagons and crew-cab Power Wagons. The company also offered a number of derivatives including a fully enclosed Power Wagon, known as the Town Wagon, in 1962.

The early years of the sixties were troubled ones for the American nation. On December 22 1961 James Davis from Tennessee became the first American serviceman killed in Vietnam and less than a month later on January 12 Operation Ranch Hand took place to defoliate parts of Vietnam using the chemical Agent Orange. The Bay of Pigs fiasco and the Cuban Missile Crisis followed as Cold War tensions heightened. In August 1963 Martin Luther King made his historic speech at the Lincoln Memorial in Washington DC and in November President Kennedy was assassinated in Dallas, Texas. Lyndon Baines Johnson the Vice-President who was with Kennedy on the trip to Texas was sworn in as the 35th US president in Dallas.

Ford had entered the sixties with another redesign for the popular F-series trucks in 1961 which included a reproportioned body. By now it had single headlights, a horizontally barred grille and a wrapround windshield. This design lasted several years into the sixties through a number of minor upgrades such as the facelift for 1962 and new grilles for 1964 and 1965. The wheelbase was lengthened while the front overhang was shortened. In 1964 the Ford name was pressed into the tailgate. Long bed variants of the F-100 and the F-150 appeared in the same year aimed at those who wanted to carry camper shells.

International Harvester had made headlines with the 1961 introduction of the Scout, one of the first

Right: *The styling of the dashboard, instruments, and steering wheel of this 1962 Chevrolet was modern and making greater use of plastic materials and technology.*

Above: *Ford continued using its "Custom Cab" designation for luxury truck models into the sixties, including its 1963 F-100 models.*

"sport utilities," although that particular term had not been coined then. It was a boxy, small pickup with rounded corners and a truck cab designed to seat three. The tailgate hinged downward and the cab roof was removable. The grille was rectangular and single circular headlights were positioned at either side. The Scout was available in both two- and four wheel drive versions, rated as a quarter-ton and known as the Model 80. It was powered by an in-line four cylinder engine and constructed around a 100 inch wheelbase. The Scout proved to be a success and in excess of 28,000 were sold in 1961. The IHC C-series pickups was a comprehensive range and upgraded versions of the earlier B-series models. The C-100/C-102 models were half-ton trucks based on a 119 inch wheelbase, C-110/C-112 trucks were three-quarter-ton trucks on a variety of wheelbases, C-120/C-122 were one-tonners also based on various wheelbases as were the C-130/C-132 models. Both the Model 80- Scout and the C-series of pickups were continued for 1962 with only minimal changes. Roll up windows were an option on the Scout and the doors were removable for off-road use and the windshield folded flat. There were similar models of the Scout for 1963 and 1964 although the pickup line was restyled.

The recreational user pickup market was growing rapidly during the mid-sixties and brought changes to the ranges offered by the likes of Chevrolet who, in 1965, introduced a 325 cubic inch V8 powered long box model suitable for demountable camper fitment.

Above: *Jason Grasseschi from Loveland, Colorado owns this flame red restored 1963 Ford. It has been fitted with custom, chrome steel wheels and radial tires.*

The company also introduced a camper special which had beefed up power train and chassis components. IHC was also aware of this growing recreational market for utility vehicles; a 1965 survey of IHC Scout buyers showed that around 75% of Scouts were purchased for non-business use and 82% of them were purchased in 4x4 form.

Looking further toward the future, in 1965 Chevrolet built another futuristic concept truck, the Turbo Titan III, with a gas turbine engine for power. It was displayed at auto shows and two years later Dodge displayed its concept truck, the Deora. The Dodge Deora was fitted with an internal combustion engine but offered car-like comfort in a pickup. In many ways these vehicles anticipated the sport-utility market by at least fifteen years. Despite Chevrolet's use of a gas turbine engine in its concept machine its internal combustion engines had plenty of miles left in them and in 1965 registrations of its trucks exceeded the 500,000 level. It was a boom time for America's number one truck maker and a year later the company sold its 10 millionth pickup. Its trucks were redesigned for 1967 and optional interior packages including the CS and CST models were offered. Chevrolet felt that this redesign was, "the most significant cab and sheetmetal styling change" in its history and certainly the trucks acquired a much more modern appearance. They appeared longer and lower and much closer to the styling of cars of the time. This was as a result of the trend towards pickups for personal transportation and leisure vehicles as well as working vehicles. The trucks were redesigned to slant inward above the waistline and to incorporate a swage line that defined the wheel wells and body sides. The area of glass in the windshield and side windows was increased and the elongated appearance was reflected in the grille that featured two long narrow rectangular panels. The new C-10 was offered on two wheelbases in both Fleetside and Stepside forms and as either a 4x2 truck or a 4x4. The only noticeable change for 1968 was the addition of additional chrome trim and badges to the trucks.

Hot on the heels of this redesign came Chevrolet's first full size 4x4, the Blazer in 1969. The suspension arrangement on the Blazer was to use tapered single leaf springs at the front and multiple leaf springs at the rear. The 4x4 Blazer base model was powered by an in-line six cylinder engine although V8s were optional as were manual or automatic transmissions, power steering, power brakes and a removable fiberglass hardtop. The colors, exterior trim, interior trim and general equipment were not dissimilar to that used on the K-10 4x4 models of pickup.

The IHC Scout was partially redesigned and upgraded for 1965, a new grille, new hood emblems and a permanently fixed windshield were among these upgrades. The windshield wipers, pedals and numerous interior details were also improved. The Scout was still available in both 4x2 and 4x4 form although 82% of the Scouts sold in 1965 were 4x4 models. The company also found that half of Scout buyers had never bought an International before and that trade-ins against Scouts included a large proportion of both sports cars and station wagons. These findings influenced IHC who marketed Scouts with increasingly luxurious interiors and for 1966 offered in-line six cylinder engines and, later in the same year, V8 options.

In 1966 the Ford Bronco appeared in three styles, roadster pickup, sport utility pickup and wagon intended to compete for sales with both the Jeep and International Harvester's Scout. The Bronco was the

Left: *Ford, like Chevrolet, was offering more luxurious interiors in its trucks in the early sixties and assemblies such as the instruments were much more stylized.*

first light utility 4x4 built by Ford since its wartime production of the GPW Jeep. While the Ford Bronco was grabbing the headlines, changes were made to the company's truck range that included front disc brakes and optional air conditioning. Also new for 1966 was the change of base vehicle for the Ranchero, instead of using the Falcon platform it was now based on the Fairlane. The F-100 truck was restyled for 1967 but continued to be available as styleside, flareside, chassis cab and platform and stake models as well as two longer wheelbase models. The F-250 remained as the three-quarter-ton variant available with as many body types and two crew-cabs, namely a styleside and a chassis cab. The one-ton F-350 was offered as a flare-side pickup and a chassis cab but also in two wheel-bases with platform and stake bed bodies. There were

Right: *Vents were introduced to the front of the 1963 Ford below the hood and above the grille. The hood ornament is heavily influenced by industrial design.*

also long wheelbase F-350 crew cabs in styleside and chassis cab variants.

Production of the Ford Bronco, International Scout and jeep models both reflected the trend toward recreational vehicle use and encouraged it, enabling owners to travel more on backwoods trails. The enthusiasm for such trips saw the arrival of specialist magazines, such as *Fourwheeler*. The development of these trucks later diverged into 4x4 and sport utilities.

The GMC trucks for 1967 were completely redesigned in both styling and engineering features. A number of safety features including seatbelts, four way flashing hazard lights and a dual braking system were included as standard. The overall shape was more slab sided and sharp edges had been eliminated in favor of rounded ones, giving a modern look to the trucks, something that was complemented by the simple radiator grille and dual headlights. Following this major redesign the changes for 1968 and 1969 were minimal although larger displacement V8s were available. By 1967 in excess of 800,000 American businesses depended on automobile use and more than 13 million people were employed in businesses that utilized buses and trucks. In the same year more than $13 billion worth of auto parts were produced for the auto industry by other industries and, reflecting the growth in recreational use of light trucks, more than 625,000 mobile homes and campers were produced. The number of mobile homes, travel trailers and truck campers produced the following year exceeded an estimated 818,000.

The war still raged in Vietnam and in 1967 the US Army was consuming 850,000 tons of supplies and 80 million gallons of gasoline monthly. At the end of January 1968 the Viet Cong launched the Tet Offensive against Saigon, Hue and other South Vietnamese cities and places such as Khe Sanh and Da Nang became committed to the pages of history books. In 1969 the US spent $28.8 billion fighting the Vietnam War and Chevrolet introduced the Blazer, a full size 4x4 ahead of a similar vehicle from Ford. The Ford Bronco and Ranchero models continued through 1968, 1969 and into the seventies in similar configurations although subsequently the body styles of the Ranchero were redesigned several times, always in keeping with passenger car like styling. Four wheel drive transmissions were available as an extra cost option. In 1968 for example the 4x4 system added an extra $645 to the cost of both the F-100 and F-250 models. In that year the production of the entire range which had been introduced in the fall of 1967 was a fraction less than 415,000 vehicles.

For 1967 the IHC Scout was marketed with three

Below: *During the sixties the Power Wagon stayed in Dodge's range of four wheel drive form. This period brochure illustrates the payload models offered and their type of use.*

Below: *By 1964 V8 engines were available in the major manufacturers' pickups either as original equipment or as extra cost options. This V8 is in a restored 1964 Chevrolet.*

different interior and exterior trim levels, Utility, Custom and Sportop. The utility models featured bench seats and painted bumpers. The custom models featured a number of interior comforts including bucket seats, armrests, sun visors, vinyl trim as well as chrome bumpers and hub caps. The Sportop featured a slanted back roof hence its name, and inside had bucket seats and other luxury trims as well as chrome moldings, trim, and bumpers. Alongside these sport utilities production of pickup trucks and crew cab trucks continued in both two- and four wheel drive form. Little was changed for 1968 but the company offered limited edition Scout models for 1969-70. The Scout Aristocrat included such features as two-tone paint and chrome custom wheels. IHC's line of conventional pickup trucks was redesigned for 1969 and the trucks were given a wide flat hood and slab-sided fenders, a design reminiscent of the still successful Scout models.

The last year of the sixties was the year that saw men, Neil Armstrong and Buzz Aldrin, on the moon as the US won the space race. It had started in 1961 when the USSR made Cosmonaut Yuri Gagarin the first man in space. Overshadowing this was some-

thing else that the US was embroiled in but seemingly could not win, the Vietnam War. In May 1969 units of the US Army and South Vietnamese forces attempted to take Hill 937 - Hamburger Hill - in the A Shua Valley east of the Laotian border. It turned into one of the bloodiest battles of the Vietnam War and provoked heavy criticism in the US as the hill had little strategic value. The Vietnam War became noted, among other things, as the first helicopter war in history and it is not stretching credibility too far to suggest that the Bell HU-1 "Huey" synonymous with images of the war was the pickup truck of the unfriendly skies. Combat troops, casualties and cases of supplies, the Huey trucked them all and more.

Above: *Mike Remley restored this 1964 Chevrolet truck from the springs up. It is finished in Chevrolet's Light Green which replaced Glenwood Green in that year.*

Right: *Mel Villegas' 1965 Ford truck is equipped with twin I-beam suspension and a V8 engine as the hood ornament (left) indicates. It has also been fitted with a camper shell, a longstanding and popular truck accessory.*

FORD
FORD

CHEVROLET
TRUCK
YP-292
19 COLORADO 64

1964 Chevrolet C10 Fleetside

This truck was completely restored from the frame up by its owner Mike Remley from Greeley, Colorado. In 1964, the year it was manufactured, this variant of the C10 series was one of 193 models in that year's Chevrolet truck range which was based on numerous wheelbases. The windshield pillars had been redesigned to slope in the opposite direction of the 1963 models but other modifications were minor. They included a redesigned grille, hubcaps, and instruments.

Specifications

Owner: Mike Remley
City: Greeley, Colorado
Make: Chevrolet
Model: C-10 Fleetside Pickup
Year: 1964
Wheelbase: 115 inches

ENGINE
Model: OHV V8
Capacity: 283 cubic inch
Ignition: Coil and points

TRANSMISSION
Type: Three speed manual

SUSPENSION
Front: Leaf sprung beam axle
Rear: Leaf sprung beam axle

BRAKES
Front: Drum
Rear: Drum

WHEELS
Kelsey Hayes 15 inch steel

TIRES
Front: 6.70 x 15 inch
Rear: 6.70 x 15 inch

PAINT & FINISH
Paint: Chevrolet
Color: Light Green

Above: *Leon Sandidge from South Dakota with his Chevy truck. Toward the end of the sixties truck styling became less curved and continued like this into the seventies.*

'He turned now to face her, exhaling a filmy cloud of cigarette smoke. 'And what happens when the money runs out?'
'Okay, then let's spend it here,' Mally said. 'Let's use it to buy a pickup truck, an old car, something unobtrusive. We can take the back roads, turn ourselves in at a precinct.'

THE GAUNTLET. MICHAEL BUTLER AND DENNIS SHRYACK (1977).

MAGNUM FORCE

THERE HAVE BEEN suggestions that the design of American automobiles reflects how good the country is feeling about itself on an almost year-by-year basis. It may be an apocryphal indicator of the nation's outlook but when viewed in the most general terms it does appear to have some credibility. Truck and car styling was flamboyant in the euphoric postwar years but decidedly lackluster in the uncertain years of the early seventies. The seventies would see President Richard M. Nixon scaling down and subsequently ending US involvement in the Vietnam War faced with ever increasing opposition to the war. At the time the US automakers were also operating numerous assembly plants around the world including 50 in South America, 60 in Europe, 17 in Africa, 40 in Asia and 27 in Oceania. Although these figures would have shifted significantly by 1973 there was concern about the volume of US domestic auto production when compared to the number of imported vehicles. In 1970 imported vehicles numbered more than 2,000,000 while domestic factories produced in the region of 8,200,000 vehicles. This latter figure accounted for 15.9% of America's steel production as well as 41.2% of the iron and 8.2% of the aluminum.

Chevrolet's Blazer was the first of the full-size, big-engined vehicles based on the idea of a shortened 4x4 pickup chassis. The Blazer first appeared during the 1969 model year in both six- and eight-cylinder engine types and was designed to be assembled from existing and proven Chevrolet and GMC light truck components that would ensure it quickly gained market place acceptance. In 1970 Chevrolet's sales were adversely affected by a UAW strike against GMC that lasted 58 days and reduced the American Gross National Product (GNP) by $9 billion. The highest specification Chevy Blazer until 1973 was the CST - Custom Sport Truck - and the Cheyenne Specification package was introduced in 1973 while a roll bar became standard in 1975. All the 4x4 models were leaf sprung front and rear. Two wheel drive Blazers were produced from 1970 onward but proved less popular than the 4x4 models. GMC put a new product - the GMC Jimmy - on the market in 1970 in order to reap some benefit from the growing recreational vehicle market. Much of its styling was taken from the GMC pickup truck range and it was virtually identical to the Chevrolet Blazer except for some trim parts. The Jimmy was available in both two and four wheel drive configurations with a removable hardtop over the

Right: *Chevrolet offered two ranges of trucks in the early seventies; the full size line as well as compact import badges such as Chevy LUV vehicles.*

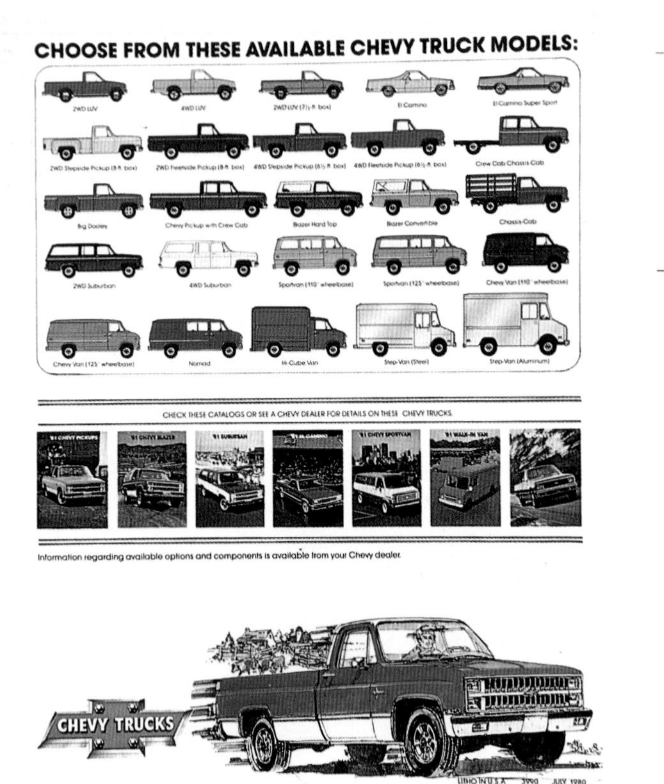

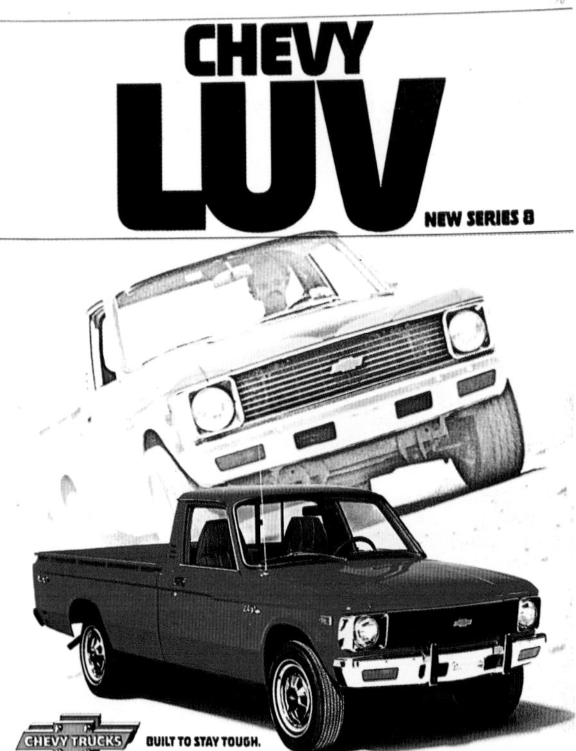

rear load bed and front seats. It was designated C1550 and K1550, the prefix varied according to the type of transmission, C indicated 4x2 models while K was 4x4. For the first years of the seventies the conventional GMC trucks continued to receive only minor upgrades for each year but they, along with the Jimmy, were restyled for 1973.

The introduction of the IHC Scout II came in 1971 and production started alongside that of the Scout and the company's conventional light truck range. The new Scout, introduced in the spring, had been redesigned and now incorporated power brakes, power steering, air conditioning, automatic transmission and a V8 engine. The body was longer and lower than that of the previous model and sales exceeded 30,000 in the first year of production. For 1972 the Scout was discontinued while the Scout II continued, upgraded only in minor details such as changes to the radiator grille. The front end of the Scout II was redesigned again for 1973 as was that fitted to the IHC range of trucks. At this time IHC was America's fifth largest truck maker behind Chevrolet, Ford, Dodge and GMC in that order.

Right from its 1966 introduction the Ford Bronco was a trend setter in the four wheel drive and sport utility sector of the truck market and the first truly mass-marketed 4x4 in the US. It featured an innovative coil spring suspension system and an in-line six cylinder engine with a V8 available as an option. The Bronco was otherwise basic and options such as power steering and automatic transmissions were not available until 1973. The Bronco lasted in almost its original form until 1977 when it was replaced by the upsized Bronco based on the Ford F-150 pickup chassis and was closer in concept to the Chevy Blazer.

Apollo 15 put wheels on the moon in 1971 when the astronauts James Irwin and David Scott drove the Boeing-constructed Lunar Roving Vehicle (LRV) several miles on the moon's surface during their mission. Closer to home the trend towards the recreational use of trucks was growing ever stronger. In 1972 the popularity of mobile homes, camper trailers,

Below: *The stylized badge on the fender of a Chevy LUV – LUV is an acronym for Light Utility Vehicle.*

truck campers, travel trailers and truck covers was such that a rise in pickup sales was recorded as part of the surge in the sale of recreational vehicles (RV). Pickups were used to haul trailers and carry camper bodies. At the time it was noted that the average RV family spent 10% of its time using the vehicle and that the family unit was made up of four persons headed by a white collar worker. This was in marked contrast to the pickup truck's distinctly blue collar heritage and, of course, its continuing use in both industry and agriculture.

In 1972 the method of construction used for the car-styled Ford Ranchero was changed. To make it bigger and stronger it now featured a separate chassis and body as opposed to the previous car-like monocoque construction with an integral chassis. A sports version was known as the Ranchero GT Sedan-Pickup and the Squire variant featured imitation wood panels along the sides and a number of other trim detail upgrades. The base models were powered by an in-line six while the base GT models featured a V8. There were numerous V8 options too that included 302, 351, 400, 429 cubic inch displacement engines as well as both manual and automatic transmissions. That year's styling changes to the conventional F-100 and F-250 truck models were considerably more lim-

CRX 416M

Above and Right: *The Chevy Blazers were based on the shortest wheelbase Chevy truck models and available in two and four wheel drive configurations.*

Left: *A 1973 Jeep truck parked alongside a 1957 model clearly shows how truck styling has evolved over a fifteen year period.*

ited and restricted to details such as a redesigned grille and interior detail upgrades.

For 1973 the F-100 and F-250 were changed considerably more than the Ranchero models. The hood was redesigned with a flatter face and the cab was longer to provide behind the seats storage and the side accent on the body was changed from being raised to indented. There were chassis cab, Flareside and Styleside variants offered. Production of the first two models totaled less than 6,000 while production of Styleside models exceeded 457,000. The F-250 models were restyled in a similar way and proportions of the production run were also similar. The total production of all three F-250 variants was approximately 198,000 vehicles. In the case of the one-ton F-350 models though the largest production was the 42,000 chassis cab models and a total of only 26,600 of all the other variants including Stylesides, chassis-cowl, platforms, parcel vans and P-400 models. This reflects the F-350's suitability for the instalation of specialist rear bodies for agricultural and industrial uses.

On January 27 1973 the signing of the Peace Accords in Paris, France brought to an end the Vietnam War. It had been the longest war in American history and the nation had suffered in excess of 58,000 killed or missing in action. The war had significant socio-economic effects on the nation which included the resignation of a president, the political turmoil it engendered and the economic problems of the early seventies. Light truck sales tapered off during 1973 due to the "gas crisis" engendered by the Arab oil embargo. The gas crisis was the occurence that both popularized the compact trucks which soon became referrred to as "minis" and opened the way for the plethora of compact Japanese imports of later years. Japanese manufacturers have since stayed away from making fullsize trucks. Although this precipitated the trend towards smaller more economical trucks in this period Chevrolet introduced a truck powered by the 454 cubic inch dis-

Below: *Don Elam's 1978 Chevrolet truck. The Greeley, Colorado resident has lowered the suspension of the truck and fitted custom wheels and an aftermarket grille.*

Below: *The truck is powered by a 350 cu in displacement V8 which Chevrolet offered as an extra-cost option. The base models were fitted with a six-cylinder engine.*

placement V8 and sold its 15 millionth truck. Despite this Ford regained the lead in sales from Chevrolet. The biggest threat to the Ford company however was no longer from Chevrolet but from imported compact trucks. In this year Japanese Datsun (later Nissan) and Toyota were selling their Li'l Hustler and Hilux trucks respectively. The latter truck was based around a 101.6 inch wheelbase and weighed 2480 pounds. The Hilux was powered by a watercooled in-line four cylinder overhead camshaft engine that displaced 120 cubic inch and produced 97 bhp @ 5500 rpm. These compact imports sold well because of their low price and both Ford and Chevrolet needed to compete. Ford sourced a Mazda truck from Toyo Kogyo of Japan. The company called it the Courier and badged it as a Ford. The Courier was built to Ford's specifications and included rubber mounts between the cab and the chassis frame. It was powered by an in-line four cylinder watercooled 74 hp engine connected to a four speed stick shift transmission. The Courier had a payload of 1400 pounds and a load bed larger than its competitors of the time. In 1972 Isuzu of Japan supplied its mini-pickups to Chevrolet, badged as Chevy LUVs. The LUV designation was an acronym for Light Utility Vehicle but also had the ring of seventies' slang to it. The LUV sold well and more than 21,000 were sold in the period between March and December 1972.

Chevrolet offered its half- and three-quarter-ton trucks with a 4x4 option from 1973, the same year as

the 15 millionth truck was made by the company. Interior trim was now offered as the Custom, Custom Deluxe, Cheyenne and Cheyenne Super range. Sales topped the 920,000 mark and despite the gas crisis the 454 cubic inch engine was greeted with immediate acclaim. The next year the interior packages were to be renamed Silverado and Scottsdale which helped Chevrolet become dominant in the light 4x4 truck market. Chevrolet's full size pickups were completely redesigned for 1973 and the new design featured squared off wheelarches, sculpted body sides, a roomier cab with more glass area and an egg crate-style radiator grille. Trim levels available included Custom, Custom Deluxe, Cheyenne and Cheyenne Super specifications. For 1974 full time 4x4 was available in the four wheel drive models through use of the NP203 transfer case in V8 models. For 1975 the 400 cubic inch displacement small block V8 was added to the list of optional engines and the NP203 transfer case became standard on all the V8 automatic transmission models. The manual models retained the conventional part time system with locking hubs. In the interior the custom trim level was deleted making the Custom Deluxe the base trim.

The Watergate scandal hit in 1974 and President Nixon resigned as the US Congress moved to

Right: *The custom aftermarket industry makes truck parts. This Chevrolet has been fitted with a custom grille and front bumper. The vehicle has been lifted nine inches.*

Below: *Jeff Murphy's custom K-10 Chevrolet stepside has modified suspension for off-road use in muddy conditions.*

BYN
919T
CEPEK

Below: *"Do it in the dirt" is one of the clichéd slogans reserved for the bumper stickers of fourwheelers modified for off-road use, such as mud-bogging competitions.*

impeach him. Gerald R. Ford became President. The year was a more auspicious one for the nation's truck makers. Dodge had redesigned its trucks at the beginning of the seventies to incorporate independent front suspension, lower and wider cabs and a new interior. The number of available options was increased to include components such as electronic ignitions. The "club-cab," an extended cab model, was an industry first. The grille was redesigned for 1974 and the Ramcharger, a 4x4 Sport Utility, was launched. Innovation continued through the seventies, full time 4x4 systems, a 4x2 Ramcharger and a dual rear wheel arrangement option for one-ton pickups of 1975 and 1976 were added. At Ford, production of both the Ford Bronco and Ranchero continued with minor changes. The styling of the F-100, F-250 and F-350 remained unchanged but an extended cab model known as the SuperCab was made available. The SuperCab was available in all three payloads and almost 30,000 were produced in the first year. Ford production of the 1974 range which had been introduced on September 1 1973 exceeded the one million mark for the calendar year surpassing Chevrolet and allowing Ford to retain its position as number one. Ford offered 4x4 variants of both the F-100 and F-250 in the same year and followed this with the F-150, a half-ton truck, which became available in 1975. A 4x4 variant of the latter pickup followed in 1976.

The IHC Scout went forward into 1974 unchanged while the pickups were given new designations becoming the 100 and 200 models for the half- and three-quarter-ton respectively. Its pickups remained in production until 1975 when the line was discontinued as was the Travelall model. Production of light trucks by Plymouth had been stopped on the outbreak of World War Two and was not resumed until 1974 when the company released the Trail Duster.

The Trail Duster was a slab sided vehicle typical of trucks of the time and available as an open machine with a choice of either a soft top or a fiberglass roof. The 1974 model was available with a 106 inch wheelbase and was a 4x4 powered by a V8 with an automatic transmission with a number of shift positions. A 4x2 variant of the Trail Duster was introduced in 1975 featuring independent front suspension in place of the driven live axle. The 4x4 model continued as before although minor trim and color changes were made and a "sport package" was offered as an extra cost option. This was repeated for 1976.

Production of an unchanged Ford Ranchero continued in 1975 although the Bronco was revised with the fitment of a stronger rear axle reflecting its popularity for off-road use. Later in the year it was further

Below: *This K-10 is described as a Scottsdale which is a specific trim level. Brushed aluminum was a common feature in the interiors of late seventies trucks.*

upgraded and fitted with disc brakes on the front axle. Exterior styling remained unchanged on Ford's range of pickups and minimal upgrades elsewhere. The range continued with only a minor facelift for 1976, America's bicentennial year. The long-running Bronco was designated the U-150 in 1978 and redesigned to standardize more parts with those of the F-series trucks and to change its appearance. Sales more than doubled in the following year and took Ford into the eighties along with the further redesigned fleet of F-prefixed trucks. In 1976 a survey in *Popular Mechanics* magazine found that 53.9% of Ford van buyers used their vehicles for recreation.

In 1977 Chevrolet saw its sales exceed one million per year. After 60 years of truck manufacture the company had made a total of 21,850,083 trucks. The LUV models had put Chevrolet firmly into the mini-truck market and were to maintain the company's strong position in this sector until the introduction of the compact Chevrolet S-10 in 1981. The 1977 Chevy LUV was available in two wheelbase lengths, 102.4 and 117.9 inches and was, according to the sales brochure for that year, "tough enough to be a Chevy." The LUV was powered by a four cylinder

80 bhp engine and according to the Environmental Protection Agency (EPA) estimates returned 34 mpg on the highway and 24 mpg in urban use. Numerous options were available including the Mighty Mike decal package, a rear step bumper, an automatic transmission, air conditioning and an AM/FM radio. Interior trim levels included the more luxurious Mikado package with a further option of high back bucket seats in place of the bench seat.

The K30 4x4 one-ton models were added to the full size Chevrolet line up in 1977 and with them came Bonus Cab and Crew Cab models. The grille was redesigned and power windows were added to the list of available options. The K prefix continued to indicate a Chevrolet 4x4 model and by 1977 it was possible to buy a GMC K3500 Crew Cab Wideside 4x4 pickup, the 4x4 option would have added $1248 to the base price. Other variations were available, such as the Desert Fox trim option of 1978 which reflected the popularity of off-road desert racing in the US. Indy Hauler trucks were also built to mark the GMC company's involvement with the Indy 500 when GMC trucks were the official speedway trucks during the famous race. In 1978 the Chevrolet truck chassis was slightly redesigned to make space to allow the fitment of catalytic converters, initially required only in California. There were a number of minor styling upgrades for 1979 that including changes to the grille. In 1977 the front end of the Ford Ranchero was redesigned to incorporate stacked rectangular headlights while production of the other Ford trucks continued in a similar style to before. The variety of options, variations and body types meant that it was possible to buy vehicles such as a F-150 Ranger XLT Flareside 4x4 Pickup. XLT was a trim level and Flareside was Ford's description of its stepside models. The Plymouth Trail Duster vehicles received a minor facelift for 1977 when the grille was redesigned to incorporate horizontal bars and vertical signal lights while the Plymouth badge was shifted from the

Below Left: *Bonanza was another trim-specification used by Chevrolet for its full-size trucks in the seventies. This is the fenderside badge.*

center of the grille to the face of the hood. The standard engine was an in-line six cylinder. IHC's Scout II remained in production however with few changes beyond a slightly different range of optional V8 engines. The production run of the Scout II would last until 1980 after which the company concentrated solely on the heavy truck market. The last years of Scouts saw the models increasingly aimed at the sport utility market although there were pickups made including the Scout II Terra Compact Sport Pickup.

For 1978, the year Americans bought an estimated 4 million pickups, the Ford Bronco was completely restyled and now closely resembled the full-size Ford pickups which had also been restyled for this model year. A rectangular grille was set higher, the amber lights were set below the headlights, and a new bumper was installed. The types of cab and transmission in 4x2 or 4x4 configurations were retained as were the F-100, F-150, F-250 and F-350 model designations. Matters continued in a similar way for 1979

Below: *Zak Wilson of Wheatland, Wyoming driving his modified Chevrolet which he has used in the truck class at local tractor pulling competitions.*

Below: *The truck features a custom nudge bar, bug screen and four KC Daylighters in pink covers mounted on the rollbar. The Chevrolet emblem is known as the "bow tie."*

although the trucks were fitted with rectangular headlights. The Plymouth models were left unchanged for 1978 after the 1977 redesign but options were offered, such as different seats, tinted glass, tilt steering column and a CB radio integrated with the AM/FM stereo. New for 1979 was the Plymouth Arrow, a down-sized mini pickup made by Mitsubishi in Japan for Plymouth. The Arrow was powered by an in-line four cylinder engine of 122 cubic inch displacement. A sport package for the same truck was also offered that included bucket seats, extra dashboard gauges, spoked sport wheels and decals.

Dodge introduced a factory custom truck in 1978 known as the Li'l Red Truck which followed from its black-painted Warlock model of 1976. Much of the seventies is remembered as the "musclecar" era and although it was almost over by 1978 the Li'l Red Truck was a fitting swansong as the first muscletruck. It was

Above: *Zak Wilson's truck is powered by a 454 cu in displacement OHV V8 engine, the largest one manufactured by Chevrolet and renowned for its performance.*

based on the D150 truck powered by a 360 cubic inch V8. The prototype had W2 cylinder heads and a Holley four barrel carburetor and would run mid-14s out on the quarter mile strip where the musclecars decided who was boss. Eventually a slightly lower performance version - it would run mid-fifteens - was offered to the public through Dodge dealers. It was finished in red, trimmed with the "adventurer" package, wooden bed details and gold decals. The truck was offered for two consecutive years, in 1978 2,188 were made and in 1979 5,118. The second year models had dual square headlights at each side of the grille while the earlier had single round lights. The later model featured a catalytic converter as the emission regulations tightened. Three Li'l Red Trucks ran in the infamous Baja 1000 desert race during 1979 in conjunction with Walker Evans, Dodge's noted off-road racer. Two made it to the finish in La Paz, Mexico while the third suffered a punctured radiator and was forced to retire.

The 1980 range of Chevrolet trucks introduced in the fall of 1979 was as large as ever and included two and four wheel drive Fleetside and Stepside models as well as two and four wheel drive Fleetside Sport and Stepside Sport models, two and four wheel drive crew cab and bonus cab models, two and four wheel drive chassis cab models for specialist rear bodies such as wrecker trucks as well as the C-10 diesel pickup and the heavy duty BIG-10 pickup. "Name the job there's a truck here to match" said Chevrolet. Four trim packages were listed, Standard Custom Deluxe, Scottsdale, Cheyenne and Silverado. The latter was the most luxurious. The eighties were just around the corner and times were changing.

BYN
919T

1979 Chevrolet K10

This half-ton Chevrolet was originally modified in South Dakota and is typical of a style of 4x4 truck built for off-road use. It features a six inch suspension lift and three inch body lift which allow the fitment of massive wheels and tires, as well as improving the approach, departure and ramp-breakover angles of the truck. The lift required new Rough Country shock absorbers and the tires required changes to the ring and pinion gears in the differentials, and a Trailmaster steering damper assembly.

Specifications

Owner: Jeff Murphy
City: London, England
Make: Chevrolet
Model: K-10 Stepside CK10703
Year: 1979
Wheelbase: 117.5 inches

ENGINE
Model: OHV V8
Capacity: 350 cubic inch
Ignition: Coil and points

TRANSMISSION
Type: Three speed auto. Two speed transfer box. Part time 4x4

SUSPENSION
Front: Leaf sprung beam axle
Rear: Leaf sprung beam axle

BRAKES
Front: Disc
Rear: Drum

WHEELS
Mickey Thompson Alloy

TIRES
Front: 44.18.5.15 Gumbo Monster Mudders
Rear: 44.18.5.15 Gumbo Monster Mudders

PAINT & FINISH
Paint: Custom
Color: Various colored panels

Above: *As Chevrolet moved into truck production for the eighties it retained the basic boxy shape of its seventies models but redesigned components such as the radiator grille. The option of diesel power was a sign of the times.*

Down at the Ford place in Clanton he was known as the last man in recent history to pay cash for a new pickup truck. Sixteen thousand cash, for a custom-built, four-wheel drive, canary yellow, luxury Ford pickup.

JOHN GRISHAM. A TIME TO KILL (1989).

THE NEW MILLENNIUM

WITH THE BENEFIT OF hindsight it seems that the eighties started in a low key way. The presidential race between Ronald Reagan and Jimmy Carter was ongoing. The Philadelphia Phillies won their first World Series baseball tournament in 98 years. The arrival of a new Chairman – Lee Iacocca – at Chrysler made the news in the automotive industry in the early eighties. As the decade opened Ford advertised its F-100 as the "first new truck of the eighties" and produced redesigned models including a number of "custom" paint options with contrasting panels. The model designations remained unchanged so it was, for example, possible to buy a Ford half-ton F-150 Custom Flareside 4x4 pickup. The Ford 4x4 models featured a new front suspension system known as the Twin-Traction Beam independent suspension. In the same year the Ranchero pickup was dropped from the Ford range. Sales of early eighties models generally dropped because of the poor state of the economy. Ford continued to sell its compact, Mazda-built Courier pickups and the company turned some of its attention to more fuel-efficient vehicles. Styling of the F-series trucks remained unaltered although there were minor upgrades including removing the word "Ford" from the front edge of the hood and instaling the famous oval blue logo in the center of the grille.

In March of 1982 the downsized Ranger pickup made its debut. With styling similar to the F-100, it had become a model in its own right rather than a trim option for an Effie and just a year later the Bronco II made its debut and more than doubled sales.

The 1979 Chevrolet range of full size trucks had been the C- and K-series pickups, crew cab pickups, fleetside sport pickups and Big Dooleys, the latter being a large capacity truck with dual rear wheels. This range continued into 1980 with only minimal changes. A range of trucks included the basic van, a Sportvan, a Nomad van and a Caravan and in addition there were the Suburban and Blazer models in two and four wheel drive variants. This range was complemented by the compact Chevy LUV and the El Camino models. In the eighties the company was to adopt a new strategy and stop manufacturing heavy duty trucks, preferring instead to concentrate on the medium and light duty markets. The Silverado models were given rectangular headlights but the major changes came in 1981. GMC made only cosmetic changes to its range of trucks as the company entered the eighties although the square patterned ice-cube

tray radiator grille remained. A styling extra-cost option that showed the direction in which auto-styling was headed was the dual stacked rectangular headlights either side of the grille in place of the single circular ones fitted as standard. The half-ton models retained an in-line six cylinder engine as standard while the other base models included a V8 engine as standard.

This program of minor upgrades continued into the 1981 models, for example, detail upgrades were made to the transmission of the 4x4 variants and the front sheetmetal of both Jimmys and pickups was redesigned to make it more aerodynamic and therefore improve fuel efficiency. New for 1982 from GMC were the S15 model trucks on which work had begun in 1978 as a response to the increasing popularity of the smaller sized imported trucks such as the Chevy LUV which was really an Isuzu with Chevrolet badges. The S15 was similar in size to the LUV and by 1983 there were 4x4 and extended cab models available. The downsized GMC Jimmy was based around the S15 and featured a tailgate and two doors on a 100.5 inch wheelbase and was a four wheel drive vehicle. The Chevrolet S-10 of 1982 was a compact that replaced the Chevy LUV and was available in two and later four wheel drive.

Above: *Crewcab models such as this Chevrolet C20 three-quarter-ton found favor with many commercial users, including the USAF, the original owner of this one.*

Right: *As well as manufacturing the Commanche trucks, Jeep experimented with Jeep-based trucks including the CJ8 Scrambler models and later this CJ10 truck.*

Jeep
Jeep
B453 XBU
GRABBER AT
GENERAL

Dodge shifted production to more aerodynamic pickups and a down-sized model, the front wheel drive Rampage, a sport truck.

New for 1984 from Ford was the down-sized Bronco II sport utility designed along similar lines to the compact Ranger pickup. The F-100 was discontinued with the F-150 becoming the base model in a range that still included the F-250 and F-350 pickups and by the middle of the decade The Ranger and Bronco II were established in Ford's range of light duty trucks along with the full size F-150, F-250 and F-350 models.

For 1984 the limited edition GMC Indy Hauler pickup, to commemorate the Indy 500 motor race, was based on an extended cab S15 model. It was one of numerous options offered that year. The full size GMC truck models continued into the mid-eighties with the same general appearance as had gone before although the program of sequential upgrades continued. Refinements were made in two areas, suspension and engine. Pickups in both wideside and fenderside variants continued to be manufactured and as a result of increasing awareness about gas-mileage, diesel options were introduced into the range.

The real news from Ford for 1986 was not about its range of pickups but the introduction of the Aerostar XL passenger van. Bronco IIs and Ranger pickups remained in the range as did the F-150, F-250 and F-350 models and after the disappointing sales of the early years of the decade Ford performed well. It had both a record sales year and regained the number one position in US auto sales. The Ford F-series ran

Above: *By the eighties, Ford's range of F-150 and F-250 models looked like this Styleside truck. The regular cab F-250 was offered with the eight foot Styleside box.*

Right: *By the beginning of the nineties, the Ford F-150 had become more streamlined and featured bumpers and headlight surrounds that were color-keyed to the truck.*

New Mexico
DRUG FREE
It's a State of Mind!

F-150
New Mexico
It's a State of Mind!

Left: *The 1993 high performance F-150 Lightning with a 351 cu in displacement V8 engine was introduced by Ford to compete with Chevrolet's sport truck, the SS. This Lightning belongs to Ray Kelly of Farmington, New Mexico.*

through the eighties, albeit with considerable changes, but remained as Ford's prime trucks intended to compete with Chevrolet during the first half of the nineties. The US economy as a whole was improving although in January 1987 it was noted that the farming economy was generally declining. It was accepted that the small independent farmer was disappearing and being driven from the land by falling prices. The number of farms was down 9% from 1975 making it the worst family farm depression in 50 years. Such a decline would, of course, affect the local economy in rural areas and decrease the number of pickups sold.

Over the course of the next decade the pickup truck market would shift considerably and sport trucks and sport utilities were to become mainstream America's major auto purchases. The compact Chevrolet S-10 was at the forefront of this trend. By 1991 the S-10 and C-series pickups and their respective Blazer and Suburban sport utility derivatives were as important as each other in the Chevrolet model line up. The nineties generation of the C- and K-series trucks were available with gas and diesel engines, short and long load boxes, regular and extended cabs and in three levels of trim, namely Cheyenne, Scottsdale and Silverado. There was a similar degree of choice for purchasers of the S-10 compact pickup with the exception of the diesel powered variant. The varying trim levels were referred to as Standard and Tahoe and there was an additional Baja off-road trim package for 4x4 models. The S-10 Blazer came in two or four door models with choice of 4x2 and 4x4 transmissions and featured an Electronic Fuel Injection (EFI) V6 engine. The trim levels offered were the same as those for the S-10. The full size Blazer was V8 gas or diesel powered with a choice of Scottsdale or Silverado trim and either two- or four wheel drive.

The APV - All Purpose Vehicle - was a new addition to the Chevrolet light truck range which included the Astro passenger truck, the Lumina APV and the Sportvan. A spectacular Sport Truck from Chevrolet completed the 1991 range although it was originally introduced in 1989 and was a truck that harked back to the musclecar era of the seventies. It was the 454 SS which was a 454 cubic inch V8 powered C1500 Fleetside pickup finished in Onyx Black.

By 1993 the 454 SS Chevrolet truck was faced with competition from Ford in the shape of the Ford F-150 Lightning which was powered by Ford's smaller displacement 351 cubic inch V8 albeit in a tuned form. Automotive magazine comparison tests of the time gave the Ford the lead in terms of all-around-use but the 454 SS Chevrolet was beyond doubt the leader in "muscle truck" terms. The Ford line up for the early nineties was comprehensive and based around three models; the F-150, F-250 and F-350 with maximum gross vehicle weights of 6250 lbs, 8600 lbs and 11,000 lbs respectively. The three sizes of truck have correspondingly increasing payloads of 2145, 3915 and 5890 lbs. There was a choice of four body styles; Regular Cab, SuperCab, Crew Cab and Flareside and three trim levels: S, XL and XLT. That accounts for 36 different pickups before the engine options are considered. There were six different engines ranging from the standard 4.9 liter in-line six through a 5.0 liter V8, a 5.8 liter V8, a 7.3 liter indirect injection diesel V8, a 7.3 liter indirect injection turbo diesel V8 to a 7.5 liter V8. That took the number of F-

Below: *The F-150 Lightning was built around the F-150 Fleetside model and badged as the performance model. This one has aftermarket billet alloy wheels.*

series variants up to 216 and then there were various transmissions. The four possibilities included manual and automatic transmissions and increased the number of F-series variants to 864. Competition with Chevrolet dictated that such a range be available to suit every customer's requirements – Chevrolet offered a similar range of choices of body styles, engine options and transmissions. New for 1994 were the driver's side airbag in F-150 and F-250 models, side door impact bars as stock across the range and a brake shift interlock system as standard on all automatic models.

While Chevrolet and Ford were still slugging it out in the full size truck class, as they had been for more than half the century, the Mini-Van trend was gaining popularity. On offer to American buyers in 1993 were the Chevrolet Astro, Ford Aerostar, Pontiac Tran Sport and Plymouth Voyager as well as Mazda and Toyota models. In the compact truck market Ford's Ranger Flareside was news. In the middle of the model year Ford introduced the Ford Ranger Flareside Splash, a sport version of the Ranger pickup. It was euphemistically described as the truck for the "under-30 crowd" and was inspired by the trend towards "personal use" pickups in states such as California. The Splash featured a restyled pickup box

Below: *The V8 engine of the F-150 Lightning was in a high state of tune and the truck was generally considered better for all round use than the muscle truck from Chevrolet.*

QUARTER CIRCLE
SALOON
SPORTSMAN'S BAR & GRILL
Budweiser
KING OF BEERS
PROUD SPONSORS OF THE NATIONAL FISH AND WILDLIFE FOUNDATION AND THE NATIONAL SHOOTING SPORTS FOUNDATION.
WELCOME HUNTERS
F250

Left: *A 4x4 Ford-250 Supercab Fleetside truck by a bar in Kremmling, Colorado. The SuperCab offers extra space within the cab without being a full crew cab model.*

that followed the stylized lines of the new Ranger - indeed the cab forward sheetmetal is 1993 Ranger - but more than hinted at stepside styling. The Flareside is V6 powered with a five speed manual transmission. Its overall appearance was enhanced with a single color paint scheme including color-keyed bumpers but offset with chrome wheels and colored graphics.

The concept of the compact truck was totally proven by the mid-nineties, its perceived advantages to the customer including fuel economy, versatility, practicality and a rugged style lacking in cars. The manufacturers were aware of the increasing popularity of this market and in 1994 the American big three makers, Ford, Dodge and General Motors Chevrolet all offered compact pickups. The trucks they made were the Ranger, Ram 50 and S-Series respectively. The Ram 50 was a rebadged Mitsubishi while at least six importers also offered trucks. The distinction between American manufacturers and importers was becoming blurred however as around 74% of the Isuzu compact trucks sold in the US in 1993 and 1994 were built at the company's plant in Lafayette, Indiana.

For 1994 Mazda started to manufacture its B4000 series trucks, a variant of the Ford Ranger, in the US. Also new for 1994 were the completely redesigned GMC S-series trucks known as the GMC Sonoma while Chevrolet retained the S-10 designation available in various trim levels in both 4x2 and 4x4 forms. There was also a major development for 1994 in the full size truck when Dodge introduced a new model Ram more than twenty years after its previous new one. The full size market was at that time divided almost exclusively between Ford and Chevrolet but the Dodge was to change that division of market shares. The Ram has styling clearly influenced by the eighteen wheeler big rigs but combines modern aerodynamic styling with the distinctive look of vintage trucks. In designing the truck Chrysler's designers were trying to leap-frog ahead of the established Chevy and Ford styling as they knew buyers of their truck would have to be tempted away from those marques. The new Dodge Ram made in Warren,

Right: *Dodge introduced the full size Ram pickup in 1994. This 1998 model has a door decal that celebrates the new Dodge and the 95th anniversary of Harley Davidson.*

Above *The styling of the Dodge Ram was influenced by that of big rigs and aerodynamic trends. The result was a truck unlike anything offered by Dodge's competitors.*

Michigan was offered with a choice of V6, V8 and V10 gasoline or a Cummins turbo diesel engines. Two- and four wheel drive transmissions, C- and K- prefixed respectively, were available and the truck was offered in three series, 1500, 2500 and 3500, half-, three-quarter and one-ton respectively. The 318 cubic inch V8 half tonner with a four speed auto box would turn a seventeen second quarter mile.

Another development for 1994 was the running at the Mesa Marin Raceway in Bakersfield, California of the first NASCAR Truck exhibition race. NASCAR racing had long been one of America's leading forms of autosport but was restricted to cars. In 1994 the exhibition race for trucks was held with only four trucks on the grid but by 1997 truck racing was almost as big as the car series. Trucks decked out in national corporate sponsors' decals represented many of the truck manufacturers including Chevrolet, Dodge, and Ford. In the 1998 season the NASCAR Craftsman Truck series was won by Ron Hornaday in a NAPA Brake sponsored Chevrolet C-1500. Hornaday was the Driver Champion and Chevrolet was the Manufacturer Champion. Chevrolet had won 15 of the 27 races in the series; Hornaday won six, Jack Sprague won five while four other Chevrolet drivers won one race each. In 1999 the C-1500 full size race trucks were superseded by the all-new full size Chevrolet Silverado. The 1500 series trucks had success in Championship Off-Road Racing (CORR) events through 1998 but it was a compact S-10 truck that claimed what is literally one of motorsport's highest prizes. Larry Ragland driving the Herzog Motorsports Chevrolet S-10 took first place in the Super Stock Truck Division at Pikes Peak. He drove the S-10 around the 156 turns on the 14,110 feet peak in 11 minutes, 37.97 seconds.

In the same year the legendary racer, Ivan "Ironman" Stewart won the 31st Tecate SCORE Baja 100 off-road race driving a V8-powered and race-prepared Toyota Tundra pickup.

By the mid-nineties the Japanese Toyota company also had constructed a factory within the US. It is in Fremont, California and for 1995 the company announced that its new compact pickup truck would

Left: *A 1998 Ford Ranger. The Ranger was the top selling compact truck in the US for more than a decade and was offered in numerous forms including the sport truck-influenced Flareside Splash model.*

be built there. The Tacoma was a refined version of its earlier truck and was available in both two- and four wheel drive forms as well as in standard cab and XtraCab forms. XtraCabs are extended pickup cabs with an area behind the seats large enough to fit a second row of seats or provide secure storage. Under a variety of names this option became available from all the truck makers during the nineties. The idea was already extant in the crew cab that had been popular for decades but now a cab with more room was offered without significantly reducing the overall size of the load bed or extending the truck's wheelbase.

As the nineties drew to a close the 1997 compact trucks from the major domestic US manufacturers included the updated Ford Ranger, the Dodge Ram-styled Dakota SLT and the Ford Ranger. This latter truck had been the top selling compact truck in the US for the past decade and for 1998 the model's wheelbase was extended by 3.6 inches to increase leg room, seat travel and space behind the seats. The available engines both base model in-line four and optional V6 were slightly increased in horsepower. The full size Ford pickups, the F-series celebrated its fiftieth anniversary in 1998. Ford's advertising of the new F-series was able to say that, "about the only thing it has in common with the typical 50-year old is the spare tire." Ford could claim to be the manufacturer of the best-built, best-selling American trucks. This claim was based on an average of consumer-reported problems at three months' ownership in a survey of Ford and competitive models designed and built in North America. The company's claim to sales leadership was based on divisional sales.

At the end of the century, the major automotive manufacturers are preparing for a new age in the evolution of pickups as environmental concerns about emissions continue to be a major issue. Chevrolet unveiled its 1999 models in the fall of 1998 and its new full size truck, the Silverado – the highest volume product GMC offers – was immediately awarded numerous accolades by the motoring media. These include the *Motor Trend* 1999 Truck of the Year, *Fourwheeler* magazine's Four Wheeler of the Year and *Sport Truck* magazine's Sport Truck of the Year.

STREET ROD
TISANA

Ford Model A Roadster

Old trucks make great street rods and Chuck Hill has owned this Ford for thirty years in which time he has driven it more than 122,000 miles. He's rebuilt it several times to keep up with the changing street rod fashions and this is its nineties incarnation. It is a combination of classic Ford parts and classic street rod items with nineties touches. The sheetmetal is old Ford. Classic street rod parts include the ARE five spoke wheels. The aluminum parts and aqua-colored paint are nineties.

Specifications

Owner: Chuck Hill
City: Longmont, Colorado
Make: Ford
Model: Model A Roadster Pickup
Year: 1929
Wheelbase: 103.5 inches

ENGINE
Model: 1967 Ford V8
Capacity: 289 cubic inch
Ignition: Coil and points

TRANSMISSION
Type: Automatic

SUSPENSION
Front: Transverse, leaf sprung tube
Rear: Mustang leaf sprung live axle

BRAKES
Front: Hydaulic disc
Rear: Mustang drum

WHEELS
American racing equipment alloy

TIRES
Front: 175/14 Radials
Rear: 255/70/15 Radials

PAINT & FINISH
Paint: Custom
Color: 1992 Ford Ranger Aqua

INDEX